CW00336303

Menorca

Compact Guide: Menorca is the ultimate quick-reference guide to this popular destination. It tells you everything you need to know about Menorca's attractions, from its wide choice of bays and beaches to its fascinating prehistoric monuments, from the streets and squares of Ciutadella to the villages and hills of the interior.

This is one of 133 Compact Guides, combining the interests and enthusiasms of two of the world's best-known information providers: Insight Guides, whose titles have set the standard for visual travel guides since 1970, and Discovery Channel, the world's premier source of nonfiction television programming.

APA PUBLICATIONS
Part of the Langenscheidt Publishing Group

Insight Compact Guide: Menorca

Written by: Thomas Gebhardt
English version by: Paul Fletcher
Photography by: Bill Wassman
Additional photography by: Pam Barrett (page 67); Gordon Singer (pages 9, 35, 92, 101, 102)
Cover picture by: Luis Real/Powerstock
Picture Editor: Hilary Genin
Maps: Polyglott/Buchhaupt
Design concept: Carlotta Junger

Editorial Director: Brian Bell
Managing Editor: Tony Halliday

CONTACTING THE EDITORS: As every effort is made to provide accurate information in this publication, we would appreciate it if readers would call our attention to any errors and omissions by contacting:
Apa Publications, PO Box 7910, London SE1 1WE, England.
Fax: (44 20) 7403 0290
e-mail: insight@apaguide.co.uk

Information has been obtained from sources believed to be reliable, but its accuracy and completeness, and the opinions based thereon, are not guaranteed.

© 2005 APA Publications GmbH & Co. Verlag KG Singapore Branch, Singapore.

First Edition 2002; Updated 2005
Printed in Singapore by Insight Print Services (Pte) Ltd
Original edition © Polyglott-Verlag Dr Bolte KG, Munich

Worldwide distribution enquiries:
APA Publications GmbH & Co. Verlag KG (Singapore Branch)
38 Joo Koon Road, Singapore 628990
Tel: (65) 6865-1600, Fax: (65) 6861-6438

Distributed in the UK & Ireland by:
GeoCenter International Ltd
The Viables Centre, Harrow Way, Basingstoke,
Hampshire RG22 4BJ
Tel: (44 1256) 817987, Fax: (44 1256) 817-988

Distributed in the United States by:
Langenscheidt Publishers, Inc.
46–35 54th Road, Maspeth, NY 11378
Tel: (1 718) 784-0055, Fax: (1 718) 784-0640

www.insightguides.com

Introduction

Places

Culture

Travel Tips

◁ **Albufera d'es Grau (p62)** The second-largest wet biotope in the Balearics, this important nature reserve attracts a wealth of birdlife.

▽ **Fornells (p66)** This oasis on the north coast is famous for its lobster dish, *caldareta de llagosta*.

▽ **Santa Maria, Mahón (p27)** As well as a busy port, the island's capital has many fine buildings. Here in the main church you can hear organ recitals in the summer.

▽ **Naveta des Tudons (p60)** This Bronze Age burial chamber is the most famous prehistoric monument in Menorca. It is thought to be the oldest roofed building in Europe.

△ **Alaior (p53)** Built on a hilltop, with narrow streets, colourful houses, decorated balconies and fine courtyards, Alaior stands out as one of the prettiest towns in Menorca. It is also the principal manufacturer of the island's most famous cheese, *Queso de Mahón*.

△ **Son Catlar (p88)**
This prehistoric village is one of the finest in all the Balearic Islands. Inhabited until the fall of the Roman Empire, it is now a UNESCO site.

△ **Cala en Turqueta (p87)** Menorca is famous for its beaches – it has one for each day of the year. Some are crowded, others remote and only accessible on foot. This shallow bay with its fine sandy beach is ideal for families with children.

◁ **Binibeca Vell (p73)**
Built in direct contrast to the high-rise hotels, this resort has won prizes for its original architecture.

◁ **Ciutadella (p35)**
With its narrow alleyways, Gothic churches, sunny squares and a beautiful harbour, Ciutadella has much to offer the visitor.

▷ **Monte Toro (p56)**
On the top of Menorca's highest peak stands a massive statue of Christ.

The Green and Blue Island

*Opposite: sailing around
Illa d'es Llatzaret
Below: cycling by Son Saura
Bottom: relaxing on
Playa Ferragut*

Menorca has always been a low-key destination for tourism, compared with the rest of the Balearic Islands. It has neither the grandiose scenery of Mallorca nor the raucous nightlife of Ibiza, but this compact, appealing little island has a largely intact, natural environment that is very special. Intimate and subtle, it casts a spell over those who want to escape the hustle and bustle of larger holiday resorts, and provides them with a real oasis.

Menorca wasn't discovered by the tourist industry until relatively late, and therefore escaped the worst excesses of the 1960s and 1970s. Now a series of strict environmental regulations have prevented developers from trying to catch up on what they thought they missed. A lot of beaches really are unspoilt; many prehistoric sites sit in isolated rural surroundings – although some of the major ones have been provided with paved access roads, souvenir stands and guardians who collect a small entrance fee. Menorca's towns have grown naturally, retaining some of their traditional industries – although agriculture and fishing support only a small percentage of the population these days. Tourist enclaves there certainly are, especially in the south, but on the whole Menorca is a peaceful haven, ideal for family holidays.

It is also the only one of the Balearic Islands to have been declared a biosphere reserve by UNESCO – a decision that has made its neighbours envious. The island known as the Isla Verde y Azul (Green and Blue Island) has finally discovered itself.

LOCATION

The first place the sun rises in Spain is above Menorca, the easternmost, and northernmost, of the Balearic Islands, which lies on 4° longitude and 40° latitude. This means that Sardinia, the Iberian peninsula, Marseilles and Algiers are all roughly equidistant from it. Barcelona,

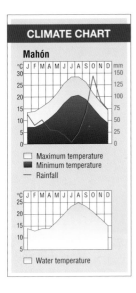

CLIMATE CHART

Mahón

°C J F M A M J J A S O N D mm
30 — 150
25 — 125
20 — 100
15 — 75
10 — 50
5 — 25
0 — 0

☐ Maximum temperature
■ Minimum temperature
— Rainfall

°C J F M A M J J A S O N D
25
20
15
10
5

☐ Water temperature

A lazy day near Son Saura

from which there are frequent ferry and air services, is 225km (140 miles) northwest. On a clear day, Mallorca is visible from the Cap d'Artrutx, the southwestern point of Menorca, and is only 20 nautical miles distant – the equivalent of 37km (23 miles).

*Menorca is only 47km (30 miles) from east to west, and some 20km (12 miles) from north to south at its widest point, but the 285km (177 miles) of coastline encircle an island that is far more varied than could be imagined from the tourist brochures. Although it is small, it has an extremely varied landscape, enchanting bays and fantastic beaches.

CLIMATE AND WHEN TO GO

The Mediterranean climate gives Menorca hot, humid summers and mild, frequently rainy winters. Visitors who come here in the peak travel season (June, July and August) usually come for sunshine and the seaside, and generally only need clothes for the beach, town visits and evening entertainment, plus sturdy shoes for the odd hike. Daytime temperatures of 30°C (86°F) and over are no rarity, and the water temperature is always above 20°C (68°F).

If you can manage it, try to come to Menorca in spring or autumn. The daytime temperatures are extremely pleasant, the sea is still reasonably warm (especially in September), the beaches are relatively empty, and the silent megalithic settlements and muted colours make visiting the island a very special experience. Serious hikers and those looking for cultural experiences will be relieved to discover that the island's interior, far from the beaches, is not as oppressively hot*.

At the end of October, when hotels and holiday resorts close down all over the island, the first rain showers arrive, heralding the start of the Menorcan winter. Around 80 percent of the annual precipitation falls between now and March. Between December and February the island is also exposed now and then to the *Tramuntana*, a cold north wind from the Pyrenees. The temperatures don't actually drop below zero at these times, but the weather is certainly a lot less pleasant. Menorca is less suitable for a winter visit than its larger neighbour. If you decide to go anyway, then take waterproofs and plenty of warm clothing.

LANDSCAPE

Put somewhat over-simply, Menorca has two main regions: the Tramuntana in the north and the Migjorn in the south. The Tramuntana is distictive for its steep coastline, bizarre rock formations and fjord-like inlets. There is not very much vegetation, apart from the forested area of La Vall near the Patjes d'Algaiarens. Slate-like, reddish-black stone tends to predominate.

Below: digging at Cala Santa Galdana
Bottom: Fornells harbour

Limestone karst regions are the most significant feature of the south of the island, which is gentler, despite its lack of trees and vegetation. The coastline is flatter than in the north, and this is where the much-praised bays and beaches are to be found. A total of 36 drainage valleys known as *barrancs* have cut their way through the Migjorn; they are biotopes, shielded from the wind, and form green oases for fertile fields or for almost impenetrable plant cover. The geological dividing line between the north and south runs roughly from the capital Maó (Mahón) in the southeast to Cala Morell in the northwest.

What's in a wall?

Menorca's stony ground delivers the building material; stones dug up by the farmers are used to build new walls or add height to existing structures. At the same time, the walls protect the fields from erosion at the hands of the *Tramuntana* wind that regularly scours the island. Watching the masons *(pedrers)* at work, you can understand why they enjoy the status of skilled artisans: the way they choose and chisel the stones, piece them all together and construct the stiles. In the 1980s, Menorca's drystone walls were declared national monuments.

Rivers or streams on Menorca very rarely have water in them the whole year round; the only one that does, in fact, is the Torrent d'Algendar; otherwise there are just a few small streams. The Albufera d'es Grau in the east of the island, however, is the second-largest marshland biotope in the Balearic Islands.

The centre of Menorca is full of fertile fields and meadows, pine groves and the odd forest of cork oak, and there is also a low range of hills which appears more like a central mountain range because the island is otherwise so flat. The highest points on the island – Monte Toro (357m/1,70ft), Enclusa (275m/900ft) and Puig de Santa Àgueda (264m/866ft) – certainly give travellers an overview.

DRYSTONE WALLS

Surveying Menorca from the top of Monte Toro, the island looks like a large patchwork quilt, divided up by a labyrinth of drystone walls known as *parets seques (see margin panel)*. The walls partition fields, surround farms and follow lanes and tracks all the way to the outskirts of Maó and Ciutadella. Depending on the time of year, the resulting landscape can be reminiscent of lush green Devon or sun-baked Malta.

Skilfully constructed, the walls taper in towards the top; and most of them are around twice the height of walls on the other Balearic islands. They are more extensive too, covering a total length of some 15,000km (9,400 miles).

OLD PATHS ON MENORCA

These days, accustomed to direct routes, we forget how difficult travelling used to be. Crossing the island from west to east, for instance, took at least two and a half days until the 18th century. The terrain was difficult, and sections of an almost 2000-year-old Roman road were used. Carts had to be loaded and unloaded so they and their contents could be heaved across ravines, because the Camí Real, or Royal Way, built after the *Recon-*

Well-forested nature reserve

quista (the 13th-century defeat of the Moors) only existed in sections and was hardly fit for a king.

All this changed when Menorca's first British governor, Sir Richard Kane (1660–1736), arrived. His practical nature turned out to be a blessing: he introduced new types of fruit and the Friesian breed of cattle, and financed water cisterns for entire villages out of his own pocket. Most importantly, he commissioned the construction of the first proper connecting road between east and west, the **Camí d'en Kane.** It's worth getting to know the 16km (10 miles) or so that still survive of this route *(see page 50).*

THE HORSES' WAY

The **Camí de Cavalls** is the name of a coastal path that was originally constructed for military horseback patrols in the Middle Ages. A ring road around the island seems impossible today because the deep ravines (*barrancs*) could not be crossed without building bridges, but in the old days dispatch riders had to make their way from one watchtower to the next to warn of enemy attacks.

In the 18th century, during the seven-year French occupation, the horses' trail was repaired in places and continued to be used by the Spanish army until the 1960s, before being abandoned. Subsequently, the island council declared several

Below: Camí way marker
Bottom: parets seques

stretches to be 'objects of public interest', and since then various sections have been renovated, notably from Cala Pregonda in the north past Cala Pilar to Cala en Carbó, and in the south from Cala Santa Galdana to Cala en Turqueta. It will be a while, however, before pedestrians and horses will be able to walk or ride round the whole island.

FLORA

Even though large areas of Menorca look green, the vegetation is actually less profuse than on the other Balearic Islands. The *Tramuntana* wind prevents some plants that flourish on Mallorca from growing here at all. There are few citrus or almond trees, but plenty of olives and oleasters, which can brave any wind.

Gnarled, windswept oleasters can often be seen clinging to the steep cliffs. Their hard wood is used by local people to make the numerous, characteristic gates that often have to be opened and closed during hikes across the island.

There are no extensive forested areas, but pines and evergreen oaks cover almost 30 percent of Menorca. Mastic trees, the resin from which is used for glue, and chest-high *macchia* – widespread in the Mediterranean – cover the whole island with their colours and aromas, as does a local variety of flowering yellow gorse.

Below: spring meadow
Bottom: traditional May dance

Up to 200 different plant species can grow in a single *barranc* here, and some of them are real botanical rarities, often only found on the Balearic Islands, such as some subspecies of carob and peony. Pomegranate trees and bushes grow primarily in the south of the island and are harvested in the autumn, together with figs and wine grapes.

Coming to Menorca in the springtime is a memorable experience: the place is a flower-filled paradise, with meadows and roadsides covered with foxgloves, crocuses and wild orchids.

> **Ornithologists**
> Ornithologists should read the book *Birds of Menorca*, published by the GOB *(Grup Ornitológic Balear)* and available in English, German, Catalan and Castilian.

Below: rugged karst scenery
Bottom: a Ciutadella woman

FAUNA

There are several kinds of reptiles and rodents here – numerous lizards, non-poisonous grass snakes, short-legged Balearic voles and a near-extinct species of wild rabbit – but Menorca is remarkable primarily for its bird-life. There are redthroats, blackthroats, nightingales, hoopoes, turtle doves and ring doves, to name but a few.

In the marshland areas of S'Albufera d'es Grau and Es Prat de Son Bou there are moorhen, waterfowl and grey herons; nearby, and along the rocky coast, kites and buzzards have their nests, and there's even a species of vulture native to the island.

To gain an impression of the aquatic life around the island the best thing to do is examine the menus outside the seafood restaurants – there's still a huge variety, even though the waters here are considered to be over-fished.

PEOPLE

The 67,000 or so Menorcans are fiercely proud of their island and the quality of life it provides. They're also hospitable and sociable, and it's easy to get involved in conversation – in a cafe, at a *branca* game (the Spanish version of *boules*) or at one of the numerous festivals that take place at different times of the year. Don't worry if your Catalan or Spanish isn't too good – the important thing is human communication.

The Menorcans have a reputation for being self-confident – this may, however, have partly

> **English influence**
> Dominated by the British for most of the 18th century, it is not surprising that an enduring colonial legacy lives on in Menorca – in the architecture, the customs, and, most intriguingly, in the local dialect. *Menorquí* is peppered with Anglicisms at every level, from the most superficial to the most profound. Some, like *vermell com un Jan* (red like an Englishman) and *ball des cosil* (Scottish dances), are colloquialisms that have worked their way in; others are direct Menorquinisations of English words. For example, *tornescru* and *bech* are the islanders' versions of the words 'screwdriver' and 'back' – totally unconnected to their Spanish equivalents of *destornillador* and *respaldo*.

originated from the need to look good in the face of their big sister Mallorca just across the water.

A historic rivalry still exists between the people of Maó and those of Ciutadella, the towns in which two-thirds of the island's population live. The British deprived Ciutadella of its capital city status in the 18th century and granted it to Maó, a reason why the latter's inhabitants are still teasingly called *ingléses* (Englishmen) now and then. Their response to this is to refer to everyone outside the capital as provincials – to the great annoyance of the people of Ciutadella, in particular.

Much of this is in good humour, however, and there are plenty of things that bind the two together: a deep religious faith (churches are still very well attended), opulent festivals for their patron saints, and last but not least, *menorquí*, their common language.

MENORQUI – THE ISLAND'S LANGUAGE

The roots of *menorquí*, one of the oldest versions of *Catalá* (Catalan), go back a long way. When Menorca was conquered by Alfonso III in 1287 and settled by Catalonian farmers and craftsmen, *Catalá* – an important language in medieval times, and of Latin origin – arrived on the Balearic Islands. The union of Catalonia and Castile raised Castilian to the level of official national language,

Everyday discourse, Ciutadella market

but the Spanish still speak a variety of regional languages, and *Catalá* is one of them. It was suppressed several times over the centuries – including during Franco's dictatorship, which lasted until his death in 1975 – during which time it could not be taught or printed. However, things changed rapidly after Franco died.

Menorquí, which still contains elements of Arabic, French and English, *now has a new lease of life. Eighty percent of lessons in the island's schools are in *menorquí* and Catalan has been the official language of the Balearic Islands since the late 1970s, although islanders all speak Spanish as well. Place-name signs have been rewritten and some villages actually renamed, which can sometimes be confusing for tourists.

Map publishers are often unable to keep up with the latest changes, and some still take you to San Cristóbal instead of Es Migjorn Gran; the names of bars and inns frequently retain the old names as well. The capital of the island took a long time to replace the name Mahón with the Catalan name Maó, but that change, too, has now been made (all the place names in this guide are in Catalan). If you do get lost, try asking *On és..?* (Catalan for 'Where is?') or *Donde està..?* (the Castilian equivalent) and you should be directed to your destination without too many problems.

Local produce ranges from gin to cheese.

ECONOMY

Claims about Menorca not being dependent on tourism because of its flourishing fish, agriculture, jewellery and leather goods industries have not been true for a long time now. The formerly important fishing fleet has dwindled to 150 boats, which only just cover the island's needs.

The situation facing agriculture is similar: it employs just 6 percent of the workforce. Dairy farming and horse-breeding tend to predominate. Cheese production (5,000 tons a year) is still important, and Queso de Mahón is still a well-known brand name beyond the island's borders – but it accounts for only a few hundred dairy farming jobs and a few dozen cheese producers.

Jewellery

In the early part of the 20th century the harbours of Menorca shipped fashion jewellery to Europe and America. British officers' wives very much appreciated the brooches and silver-studded handbags, and Menorcan jewellery was soon a regular sight in the world's fashion shops. In those days a workforce of around 3,000 processed 15,000kg of silver annually to keep up with demand. All that is now history, of course. Not much remains of the once-flourishing trade, though the fine work of the island's coppersmiths and silversmiths in Alaior and Ciutadella is still an integral part of the SEBINE fashion jewellery fair, held in May every year.

Checking departure times

Spain's entry into the European Union in 1986 also imposed quota limitations: cattle numbers had to be reduced by around one third to 25,000.

The traditional footwear and leather goods industry manufactures products for Italian and French companies, and also supplies other European countries with brands such as Pons Quintana and Gomila, but it is relatively small.

The jewellery industry is having to combat cheap imports from the Far East or competitive products from Portugal and the Spanish mainland, and production has long since been limited to a handful of manufacturers or cottage businesses.

TOURISM

Economic diversity has been enhanced by Menorca's status as a UNESCO biosphere reserve, awarded in 1993, with the aim of sustaining tourism development within the framework of conservation and support for local industry. Even so, Menorca has not been immune from the Balearics' tourism explosion. In 1950, the island had just 200 hotel beds; now there are 40,000 and around a million visitors a year. Apart from the 18 percent of the population who work in banking, 56 percent of Menorcans live directly or indirectly from tourism: waiters, hotel owners, windsurfing instructors, sales people.

More than half the holidaymakers come from the UK, followed by those from Germany, Spain and Italy. Since the beach and suntan season is limited to the period between May and September, 24 percent of Menorcans are unemployed during the winter months. The wages and tips earned during the holiday season often have to tide tourism workers over into the next one. Menorcans are becoming increasingly concerned about accelerating tourist resort development, as well as the high price of land, pushed up by foreign home ownership. The island government has taken steps to protect the environment by imposing strict building regulations and has created a natural park around S'Albufera d'es Grau. However, an eco-tax, imposed in 2002 on hotel occupants, was considered detrimental to the tourist industry and was abandoned the following year.

POLITICS AND ADMINISTRATION

When Franco died in 1975, Spain was radically reorganised: the country received a democratic constitution and was transformed into a parliamentary democracy. Under a Statute of Autonomy in 1978 the Balearic Islands were one of 17 regions to be given a measure of autonomy. In 1983, they officially became Comunidad Autónoma de las Islas Baleares, with Palma de Mallorca as their capital. There the *Govern Balear* – the provincial government – has a considerable amount of say in the islands' affairs, especially in matters concerning culture, education, tourism, energy management and construction.

Each island also has its own *Consell Insular*, (island council), with powers ranging from the control of archaeological investigations on prehistoric sites to issues regarding tourism, construction and social policy. Municipal matters are taken care of by the mayors and councils of eight Menorcan administrative districts.

The winner of the most recent regional elections in the Balearics was the Conservative PP (Partido Popular), which means that the islands are now politically to the right of the central government of Spain.

Below: local and EU flags
Bottom: a crowded Cala Santa Galdana

HISTORICAL HIGHLIGHTS

ca 5000BC First signs of settlement on Menorca by gatherers and fishermen from southern France and eastern Spain who constructed large cave complexes.

From 2000BC Walled settlements and stone structures are built by the megalithic Talayot culture: they leave fortified towers *(talayots)*, table-shaped cult sites *(taulas)*, and burial chambers *(navetes)*, shaped like upturned boats.

ca 1000BC Phoenicians begin trading with the island, which they call Nura (Island of Fire), probably deriving from warning fires along the coast. The settlements of Mogona (Mahón) and Iamnona (Ciutadella) date from this time.

ca 400BC The Balearic Islands are taken over by the Carthaginians. The countryside is exploited for agriculture; oil and wine are the principal products.

205BC Carthage falls to Rome after the Punic wars. Romans annex the Balearics.

123BC Mallorca and Menorca occupied by the Romans. Menorca receives the name Balearis Minor.

AD200 Balearics convert to Christianity.

426 Vandals devastate the islands, and persecute the Christians. Trade declines.

534–902 Vandals defeated by Byzantines; Christianity restored; the Balearics become part of the Byzantine Empire.

902 The islands conquered by the caliphs of Cordoba. Around 1000, Medina Minurka (Ciutadella) is made the capital. The Balearics remain under Moorish rule until the 13th century, and flourish culturally. Menorca becomes a fortified base for Mediterranean pirates.

1015 The collapse of the caliphate of Cordoba; the Balearics annexed to the small Muslim kingdom of Denia.

1087–1114 The islands become an independent kingdom, which is known as the *taifa* of Mallorca.

1203–29 The Balearics fall into the hands of Almohadian tribes from Algeria and Denia. Resulting political instability lays the islands open to foreign occupation.

1229 Jaume I of Aragon occupies Mallorca; he conquers Menorca in 1232.

1276 Death of Jaume I; the kingdom is divided. Menorca becomes part of the newly created Kingdom of Mallorca.

1287 Reconquest of Menorca by Alfonso III of Aragon and Catalonia.

1298 Alfonso's successor, Jaume II of Aragon, returns the Kingdom of Mallorca (including Menorca) to his exiled uncle, Jaume II of Mallorca.

1312–24 The reign of Jaume III brings great economic prosperity to the islands.

1344 Troops of Pedro IV of Aragon invade and reincorporate the Balearics into the Kingdom of Aragon. Immigrants from Catalonia arrive, bringing their language with them; the towns of Alaior, Es Mercadal and Ferreries are founded.

1349 Jaume III tries to recover the Kingdom of Mallorca but dies in battle.

1469 Marriage between Isabela of Castile and Ferdinand of Aragon unites the Spanish crowns: the Catholic Monarchs rule all of Spain, including the Balearics, from 1479.

16th century The island is attacked on numerous occasions by Ottoman and Moorish fleets. Spanish king, Charles V, has fortresses built to protect the towns.

1558 Following a 10-day siege, Ciutadella is almost completely destroyed by a 15,000-strong Turkish army.

1708 Menorca is seized by the British during the War of the Spanish Succession – a move that is sanctioned by the 1713 Treaty of Utrecht.

1722 The British shift the capital from Ciutadella to Mahón (Maó).

1756–63 French troops occupy the island and found the town of Sant Lluís. Under the Treaty of Paris, Menorca is handed back to Britain.

From 1763 Numerous fortifications are built, including the Georgetown garrison, later to become Villa Carlos and then Es Castell.

1781–2 Franco-Spanish troops land on Menorca, and the island falls to Spain. All fortifications removed. Economic decline sets in.

1795 The diocese of Menorca is established, with Ciutadella as its bishopric.

1802 The Treaty of Amiens gives the island to Spain once and for all.

1803–13 The War of Independence against Napoleon. Refugees arrive, provoking social and political unrest.

First half of the 19th century Numerous Menorcans emigrate to Northern Africa, especially Algeria.

1879–98 Period of social and commercial success ends when the phylloxera virus destroys the wine industry. Eco-

nomic decline results in widespread emigration to the mainland and to the USA.

1936 Franco leads uprising against Republican government. Mallorca and Ibiza support Franco' but Menorca backs Republicans in ensuing Civil War. The island falls to Franco's troops in 1939.

1939–45 Spain plays no part in World War II.

1953 The first charter plane lands on Menorca and the age of tourism begins.

1975 On Franco's death, Spain becomes a constitutional monarchy under King Juan Carlos I.

From 1978 Spain gets a democratic constitution. The Balearics become one of 17 autonomous regions, with Palma de Mallorca as the capital. Menorca's Island Council is formed in 1979.

1986 Spain joins the European Community (later the European Union).

1991 The Balearic parliament passes an environmental protection act; one-third of Menorca turned into a nature reserve.

1993 UNESCO declares Menorca a biosphere reserve.

From 1997 Increase in reconstruction work on cultural monuments. Steps taken to limit damage inflicted by mass tourism and take the industry upmarket.

1989–2001 The economy prospers; the Balearics enjoy the highest per capita income in Spain

2002 Spains adopts the euro.

2004 Socialist Party wins Spanish general elections but right-of-centre Partido Popular holds power in the Balearics.

Map on page 24

1: Maó

In 1928, a glowing account of Maó, by Roy W. Baker, then the American consul in Barcelona, appeared in the *National Geographic Magazine*. He described the Menorcan capital as 'a maze of blinking alleyways leading up and down hill, lined with bright dolls' houses'. Maó, located at the end of a long, narrow bay, was at that time one of the finest harbours in the Mediterranean. Baker also mentioned that the place had the feel of an English provincial town.

A VERY BRITISH TOWN

Preceding page:
Ciutadella by night
Below: Maó street sign
Bottom: Maó harbour

At first sight this little city, with a population of 22,000, seems more restrained than one would expect in these latitudes. This is probably because it has had several different rulers in the past, due to its strategic location. The British, who held Menorca throughout the 18th-century and made Maó the island's capital, introduced several very English elements: sash windows, green shutters and brass door knockers among them. There's even a gin distillery. The two main churches were also built during the years of British rule. In many ways, however, everything is very Spanish, as you will find if you go to the market in the Claustre del Carme, for example *(see page 30)*.

PLAÇA REIAL

HISTORY

If the legend is true, Maó owes its existence to Mago, the brother of Hannibal, who visited the island to recruit Menorcan slingers – experts at fighting with the slingshot – in around 205BC. Etymologically it is more likely, however, that the name derives from the Phoenician word *maghen*, meaning 'fortification'.

After the Phoenicians and Carthaginians, it was the turn of the Romans to marvel at the harbour's perfect strategic location. In the 1st century AD they made Magona into Portus Magonis, and it soon became an important harbour town. The Romans also built a road to *Iamnona*, today's Ciutadella. The Romans were followed by the Byzantines, and then the Moors, who were driven from Menorca in 1287 by Alfonso III of Aragón.

The 16th century brought renewed attacks by Moorish and Ottoman pirates, and Maó lost many of its inhabitants as a result. Charles V had a further wall built to protect the harbour entrance. On their next visit to the island the Turks decided to move on to Ciutadella, which they duly razed to the ground *(see page 35)*.

(see page 35)

CHANGES IN GOVERNMENT

In 1708, during the War of the Spanish Secession, the British occupied Menorca, and in 1722 they elevated Maó to the status of island capital. Under Sir Richard Kane, the first British governor, a well-surfaced road was built from the city to Ciutadella. The harbour was extended, and new fortifications such as Fort Marlborough were built. British influence is visible everywhere in Maó today, especially in the architecture; the French were only here for eight years and little of their influence remains.

In 1802, after Menorca had fallen to Spain once and for all under the terms of the Treaty of Amiens, the once-popular metropolis was forgotten for several decades. Today, however, Maó is the economic heart of Menorca and still the capital. The new Spanish constitution of 1978 gave autonomy to 17 regions and five years later the islands off-

Strategic location

Maó has always been at the centre of the island's turbulent history. Its long, deep harbour has provided protection for the city's rulers, but also borne the brunt of numerous invasions. The result is a city whose influence is greater than its size.

Rider at the festival of the Vierge de Gràcia in the Plaça de la Constitució

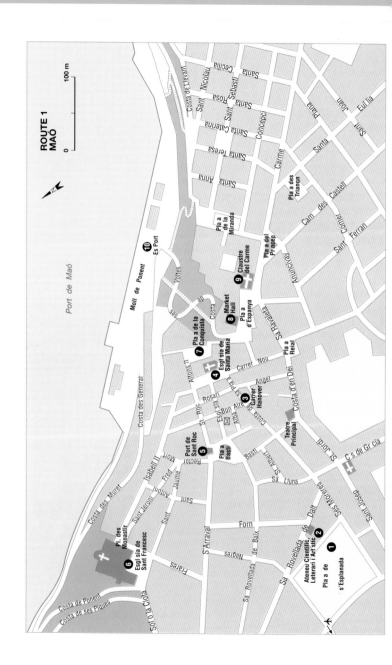

ROUTE 1
MAÓ

Port de Maó

ficially become the Comunidad Autónoma de las Islas Baleares. Since then Menorca's fortunes have been steered to a large extent from Palma de Mallorca. The *Consell Insular* in Maó only has responsibility for archaeological, agricultural, constructional and social issues.

SIGHTS

The large **Plaça de s'Esplanada ❶** was formerly used by the British as a parade ground. Most of the important access streets end here, an underground car park swallows up visitors' cars, and the bus terminal is just around the corner. The rectangular, palm-lined square is a good place to observe Menorcan life at any time of day. A market is held here onTuesday and Saturday, drawing visitors in from the surrounding resorts.

Every day, from early morning, you can see old people sitting in cafés such as the Cafeteria Consey or on stone benches beside hibiscus bushes, chatting together or reading the latest edition of *Menorca – Diario Insular*. Children clamber up climbing frames, while soldiers guard the formerly British-owned barracks. An obelisk commemorates those who fell on the Nationalist side in the Spanish Civil War (1936–39). If you are looking for information, go to the tourist office just off the eastern side of the square in Carrer Sa Rovellada de Dalt.

Below: life in Maó
Bottom: altarpiece, Maó

CULTURAL CENTRE

Opposite the tourist office is the **Ateneu Cientific, Leterari i Artístic ❷** (Jul–Sept, Mon–Fri 10am–2pm; check with tourist office for winter hours; free), an old-fashioned place that is home to Menorca's most important cultural association. It contains a library with a reading room and numerous tomes on the island's history, a collection of landscapes and still-lifes, ceramic plates and wall tiles. You will have to ask if you want to see the antechamber full of stuffed native birds, fish in formalin, seashells and minerals that are kept under lock and key.

Map on page 24

Organ recitals
Try to go to an organ recital in Santa Maria if you get the chance. In the summer months there are recitals every day but Sunday at 11am, and international organists perform during the evening. CDs are also on sale as souvenirs .

The shopping street Carrer de des Morreres is very busy all year round and souvenir, fashion and food shops vie for the custom of local people and tourists. A bust commemorates Dr Mateo José Orfila (1787– 1853) who was born at No. 13 and went on to found modern toxicology and pathology in the distant Institut Pasteur in Paris. He also invented a method of tracing arsenic.

In the narrow alleyway of Costa D'en Deià you will find yourself confronted by the **Teatre Principal**, with a statue of a discus thrower outside. The Italian architect and tenor Giovanni Palagi designed the original building and the curtain first rose here in 1829, before that of the Teatro Real in Madrid. Except in Opera Week (the week preceding Easter), very little remains of the glorious days when Italian ensembles began their operatic tours of Spain in Maó, but the theatre has recently been given a complete make-over and there is a full programme of performances.

CARRER HANOVER

Back to the busy shopping street, which becomes the steep ★ **Carrer Hannover** ❸ (also known as Costa de Sa Plaça). The (misspelt) name is a reminder that the English throne in the mid-18th century was occupied by members of the House of Hanover, and a Hanoverian regiment was garrisoned at the Plaça de s'Esplanada.

This street has some extremely tempting shops, but its architectural style should not be overlooked as it is very English and typical of Maó. There are sash windows on every house and door handles that need to be pushed downwards – the Menorcans call them *pestells*. The bow windows are known as *boinders*, and a particularly ornate one can be seen at the corner of Carrer Bastio.

The street passes through the little Plaça Colom, with its statue of a flower girl, framed by four palm trees, four benches and four basins. There is a good bookshop here (Fundació) with an interesting selection of Balearic and Menorcan literature. Continue on for a short way and you will reach the Plaça de Sa Constitució.

A decorated Plaça Colom

SANTA MARIA

The Plaça de Sa Constitució is dominated by the **★★Església de Santa Maria ❹** (daily 7.30am–1pm, 6–8.30pm; free), which was built above the remains of an older structure between 1748 and 1772, in honour of the patron saint of Maó. The neo-classical façade is relatively unpretentious, while the single-aisled nave is Catalan Gothic and there are baroque and rococo flourishes around the altar.

Star Attraction
• Església de Santa Maria

The most important object is the mighty organ, a masterpiece of its kind. In 1809 a Maó merchant commissioned the renowned Swiss organ-maker Johann Kyburz to construct it, and a year later it arrived on the small Mediterranean island. The instrument became famous for its uncannily realistic *vox humana*, and after extension and renovation work it now has 3,210 pipes, 215 of which are wooden. From June to October short organ concerts are held from Monday to Saturday at 11am (small fee).

Below: the Santa Maria organ
Bottom: ceiling, Santa Maria

THE TOWN HALL

The other fine building in this square is the **Ajuntament** (Town Hall), built on what was originally the site of a medieval fortress, of which only a few remains of foundation walls in the cellar survive. The façade is crowned by a bell wall and clock

Map on page 24

Below: Town Hall entrance
Bottom: Arc de St Roc

tower, which was donated to the city by the first British governor, Sir Richard Kane *(see page 11)*. The interior of the Town Hall is British in style too: alongside portraits of Spanish governors and a Roman signet stone showing that Portus Magonis received civic rights in the 1st century AD, there is a portrait of the English king, George III (1738–1820). The figures outside the main council chamber wearing Menorcan folk dress are almost 3m (10ft) high, and are carried through the streets of Maó during festive processions.

PORT DE SANT ROC

Walking down the Carrer de Sant Roc, you will see the late 15th-century ★ **Port de Sant Roc ❺**. This is the only one of Maó's mighty medieval town gates to have survived from the former fortifications and is now a national monument. It once marked the start of the long and arduous route to Ciutadella, and was also the town boundary until the 18th century. In a niche above it is a sculpture of St Roc, who is believed to have saved Maó from an outbreak of plague.

A few yards left is the **Plaça del Bastió**, where restaurants with awnings provide a welcome rest. The *tapas variadas* are good here and children will enjoy the rocking-horses and climbing equipment in the middle of the square.

TOWARDS THE MONASTERY

The Carrer des Rector Mort leads into what used to be the smartest suburb of Maó, which began spreading beyond the old town walls back in the 17th century. Just next to the narrowest building in the capital, the Carrer Fred branches off. No shop windows or advertisements break the brownish-yellow façades here, but a touch of colour is added by washing on the lines stretched across the street.

You soon come to Carrer d'Isabell II, then to the Plaça d'es Monestir, lorded over by the ★ **Parròquia de Sant Francesc ❻** (daily 10am–noon, 5–7pm, except Thur pm), which was built in 1791–92 as the church of a Franciscan monastery. Above the entrance doorway is a baroque *Annunciación*, and All Saints' Chapel inside illustrates the churrigueresque-baroque style, with highly ornamental decoration, which is quite rare on this island.

All that remains of the former monastery is the cloister, which houses the extensive historical and archaeological collections of the ★★**Museu de Menorca** (Apr–Sept, Tues–Sat 10am–2pm, 5–8pm; Oct–Mar, Tues–Fri 10am–2am; entrance charge). Highlights include *talayotic* finds as well as a Gothic stone with an inscription in memory of the *reconquista* of Menorca by Alfonso III, together with Islamic tiles and Spanish and British ceramics; modern sculpture is displayed in the courtyard.

PLAÇA DE LA CONQUISTA

Go back down Carrer d'Isabell II, and you will see the colonial-style palace of the former British governor, today the seat of the Gobierno Militar. There are several other smart mansions. One of the finest, at No. 42, is the headquarters of the biggest nature conservation society in the Balearic Islands. You will also pass a wonderful candle shop, the Cereria Abell, before arriving back at the Església de Santa Maria. The nave of the

Star Attraction
• Museu de Menorca

Harbour view
From the peaceful square in front of Sant Francesc there's a fantastic panoramic view of the harbour, and not far away the narrow alley called Costa d'es General leads down to the waterside.

Sant Francesc

Map on page 24

Map on page 24

👁 **Important collection**
The Carmelite monastery houses the **Hernandez Mora Collection**, once the property of historian and philologist Dr Hernandez Mora, with historic engravings of the Mediterranean region, paintings, old maps, numerous items of furniture and also a library (Mon–Sat 10am–1pm; free).

Below: Alfonso III monument
Bottom: market stall

church separates the Plaça de la Constitució from the **Plaça de la Conquista** ❼, and the building dominates both squares. The patrician house Ca'n Mercadal contains the municipal library, and outside the rear entrance to the church is a monument to Alfonso III. At the end of the small cul-de-sac called Pont d'es Castell – the name is a reminder of the drawbridge that was once located here – there is a fantastic view across the harbour.

MARKETS AND CLOISTERS

Anything the fishermen catch in their baskets and nets is up for sale at the ornate ★ **Mercat** ❽ on the Plaça d'Espanya. Pike, flounder and stickleback lie on ice, and crustaceans – *mariscos* – are piled high. If you are in self-catering accommodation and in a position to buy, you'll find you usually get a free handful of fresh parsley.

Next door stands the neo-classical **Església del Carme**. The largest church in Maó, it was built between 1726 and 1808, when it lay outside the city walls. The altar has some interesting medallions depicting the life of the Virgin Mary. The Carmelite monastery to which the church belonged served as a judicial building for some years after it was deconsecrated in 1835. The adjoining cloister, the **Claustre del Carme** ❾ is home to the town's main ★★ **fruit and vegetable market**, plus a number of shops selling leather goods and craft work. The ecclesiastical architecture and the intense colours and smells of a Mediterranean market make an an unusual mixture. On summer evenings concerts are sometimes performed and films screened in the centre of the cloister. The Café Bar Mirador, off to one side, has a sunny terrace and wonderful harbour views.

On the small Plaça de Miranda beyond the church, in a fine and commanding position above the harbour, is a monument to Almirante Augusto Miranda, honoured with a bust, an anchor and a cannon for having founded the naval station at Maó in 1916. Back in the Plaça d'Espanya, you can follow the curved road or the broad steps of **Costa de Ses Voltes**, lined by shrubs and palms, to the harbour below. Street musicians, hair-braiders and stalls selling sarongs and sandals cluster at the bottom of the steps, especially when cruise ships are in port.

The Harbour

Local people refer to their harbour simply as ★★ **Es Port** ⑩, and it is undoubtedly the biggest attraction of the island's capital. This natural harbour is 6km (4 miles) long and up to 1km (½ mile) across. Maó was considered the safest harbour in the Mediterranean by Andrea Doria, Admiral of the Spanish Navy. But in the years since its naval days – the British kept most of their Mediterranean fleet here until 1802 – the harbour has had to earn its living in different ways.

Instead of destroyers, cruise ships, ferries and freighters visit the harbour and the jetty is lined by hundreds of white-sailed yachts from all over the world, all contributing to a picturesque scene; while the mariners' pubs and dives have been turned into elegant restaurants, bars and discos.

Boat Tour

The best way of getting a view of Maó from the sea is to take a round trip of the harbour. Glass-bottomed boats depart from the main harbour area

Star Attractions
• Es Port
• fruit and vegetable market

Below: local sailors
Bottom: Mediterranean cruise-liner

Map on page 24

Sampling the gin

The Xoriguer Distillery (open daily; closed 1–4pm) produces gin and various gin-based liqueurs in its old-fashioned copper stills. Gin has been made on Menorca since the late 18th century, but its popularity with British sailors helped ensure its survival. Visitors are encouraged to taste and buy; try the gin-and-lemonade mix, *pomada*, a Menorcan version of gin and tonic .

Below: hanging out in Maó
Bottom: gin was introduced
by the British

on an hourly basis in summer. The trip leads past the **Illa del Rei**, or King's Island, with its former naval hospital, and the **Illa de Llazteret** with the ruins of the medieval quarantine station, which today is used as a holiday resort and conference centre. The harbour could quickly be sealed off in times of danger, as is clear from the ruins of the fortress of Sant Felip near Es Castell and the **Fortaleza de la Mola** (guided tours; tel: 971 362 100 for details) on the north side of the harbour, known simply as S'Altra Banda (The Other Side). Until 1968 *the fort* was one of Franco's most notorious military prisons.

Not far from here is the Finca Sant Antoni, a rusty-red colonial manor house in 18th-century colonial style, sitting above the northern part of the harbour. It is usually known as **Golden Farm** and sometimes called the Nelson Museum, but it is privately owned and cannot be visited. The story connecting it with Admiral Horatio Nelson (1758–1805) is misleading. Legend has it that he spent several romantic weeks here with his mistress, Lady Emma Hamilton, but, in fact, he made just one brief visit to Menorca – and he was alone.

ATTRACTIONS FOR ALL

Back to the harbour now. The promenade running west is called Moll de Ponent (Western Quay) the busier stretch to the east is Moll de Llevant (Eastern Quay). The numerous and varied restaurants *(see page 108)* are joined by some interesting shops. At Hermanos Lora Buzón (Moll de Ponent 10) and S'Alambic (Moll de Ponent 35), you can buy some original pottery; at S'Abarca (Moll de Llevant 21), Menorca's typical sandals *(see page 113)* are made to order on the premises; and the local Pou Nou brand of attractive cotton casuals are available in several stores.

The art nouveau building that used to be headqaurters of the electricity company is the **Destileria Xoriguer** (Moll de Ponent 93), which distils and sells Menorcan gin *(see margin panel)*. The crush for tastings begins early in the morning when the first cruise boats dock.

EXCURSIONS FROM MAO

Apart from Maó's main beach, the Cala Mesquida and the dreamy little bay of Cala Murtar (both to the north of Cap de la Mola), there are some other attractive destinations near the city.

Star Attraction
• **Ermita de Gracia**

ERMITA DE GRACIA

The ★★**Ermita de Gracia** and the municipal **Cimenterio**, both on the southwestern edge of Maó, can be reached after a longish walk.

The unpretentious monastery church was built between 1436 and 1491 and consecrated to the Virgin Mary, but was used for all kinds of purposes after that. First it was utilised as a military hospital by the French and then the Spanish, and in the 18th century it even contained a powder magazine. The snow-white façade dates from 1733, and the nave is Gothic. The maritime votive offerings inside were donated by mariners and fishermen rescued from shipwrecks; they were especially grateful to Nostra Senyora de Gracia, whose statue can be seen in a niche behind the altar.

The peaceful cemetery, with its rows of tombs, is also worth a visit. Anyone who could afford to do so had veritable palaces built above their tombs, as a mark of their prestige.

Below: Cala Mesquida
Bottom: Ermita de Gracia

Map on page 49

TREPUCO

Less than 2km (1 mile) from the church (heading south) is the megalithic settlement of **Trepucó**. The *talayot* (fortified tower) here is one of the largest on Menorca, and the *taula* (table-shaped stone) is certainly the most magnificent pre-Christian sacred monument on the Balearic Islands. The supporting stone is 4.2m (13.7ft) high and covered by a 3.5m (11.5ft) by 1.5m (5ft) stone slab; there are also numerous menhirs scattered around the temple site.

ES CASTELL

Below: taula at Trepucó
Bottom: crossing the Plaça de s'Esplanada

★★ **Es Castell** (pop. 5,400), located on the southern edge of Maó's broad harbour, and virtually part of the city, is certainly worth devoting a whole day to. It has two inlets, Cales Fonts and Cala Corb; the most easterly town in Spain it is the first to get the morning sun. It was founded in the late 18th century when the British built a garrison town near the fortress of Sant Felip and named it Georgetown, after George III. Under the Spanish it became Real Villa de San Carlos (Villa Carlos), in honour of the king of Spain. Finally the present name, which simply means The Castle, stuck, because of its proximity to the fortress.

As in Maó, life in Es Castell revolves around a central square that was a former parade ground. The town's history is reflected in the architecture here. On the square are the Ajuntament (Town Hall), a barracks containing the **Museu Militar** (Mon, Thur, first Sun of month 11am–1.30pm; entrance charge), and numerous cafés and bars.

Inviting café terraces line the beautiful bay of Cales Fonts, which has all the atmosphere and charm of a traditional fishing harbour. Many of the shops and restaurants are built into caves in the walls around the harbour, with a wide range of items on sale, from ceramics to *abarcas*.

A short distance further along the main road from Maó is pretty little Cala Sant Esteve and **Fort Marlborough** (Tues–Sun 10am–1pm, 5–8pm; free) an 18th-century British fort with a Martello tower and underground galleries.

2: Ciutadella

Ciutadella, Menorca's former capital, is very different from British-influenced Maó. Large, splendid *palazzi* and an impressive cathedral are as much a part of the scene here as shady arcades, beautiful sun-soaked squares and an undeniably picturesque harbour.

The ★★★ **Old Town** of Ciutadella was built in the 16th and 17th centuries, after a 15,000-strong Turkish army had completely destroyed all previous structures, and it is remarkably homogeneous. An obelisk in the Plaça d'es Born commemorates the Turkish attack. This broad square is lined with bars where you can stop for a *ginebra* – the Menorcan gin – or relax over a *café con leche*.

Ciutadella (pop. 21,000) is a fascinating place. Its narrow alleyways are so tempting that it's very easy to ignore maps and guidebooks and simply set off exploring alone. Wherever you end up is bound to be pleasant and you are unlikely to get lost for long.

HISTORY

The town's origins date back to the Phoenicians, who founded a trading post in the west of the island and called it *Iamnona*. They were followed

Map on page 36

Star Attraction
• Es Castell

> **Menorca's Little City**
> As the crow flies, Ciutadella is less than 50km (30 miles) from the Mallorcan coast; at dusk the mountains of Mallorca turn pink on the horizon. So perhaps it should come as no surprise that the old town, with its Gothic churches and honey-stone façades, is rather like a miniature Palma. This is, after all, what the city's name implies. Palma's alternative name is Ciutat de Mallorca; Ciutadella de Menorca means 'Menorca's little city'.

Ciutadella kids

Map
below

by the Romans, and the settlement was fortified and extended, but for a long time it lay in the shadow of *Portus Magonis*, today's Maó, in the east of the island. For a short while in the 5th century, Ciutadella was one of the first bishoprics in the Balearic Islands.

When the Moors took over power the town became known as *Medina Minurka*, and as capital of the island it was the seat of the Arab governor for centuries. In 1287 the Christian king Alfonso III of Aragón entered the city via the Porto de Maó, today's Plaça de Alfons III *(see page 47)* after a three-day victorious march, and named it Ciutadella de Menorca, which means Menorca's little city.

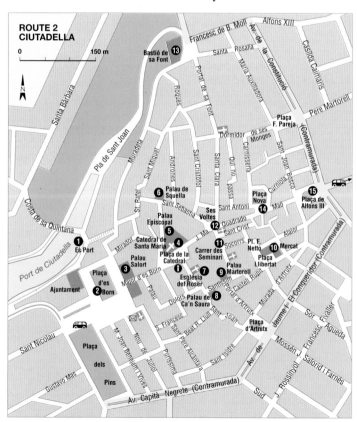

ROUTE 2
CIUTADELLA

0   150 m

RISEN FROM THE ASHES

New town walls and bastions now appeared, based on the fortifications at Perpignan, and attacks by Moorish and Turkish pirates could at first be repelled. A black day in the town's history was 9 July 1558: after nine and a half days' siege, a 15,000-strong Turkish army entered Ciutadella, plundering and murdering, and finally leaving with 3,500 hostages. All that remained of the town was dust and ash.

This is why the reconstruction in the 17th century was more like a re-foundation. Magnificent *palazzi* were built in the Catalan and Italian styles. But in the meantime, Maó was becoming increasingly important for military reasons, and in 1722 the British turned Ciutadella's rival into the island's capital. To soothe ruffled feelings, Ciutadella was made a bishopric in 1795. In the mid-19th century large sections of the town's fortifications were razed to the ground to make way for more residential land. Today the town lives from the leather and shoe-making industry, but mostly from tourism, and the harbour is only of regional importance.

> **Shopping for shoes**
> Ciutadella's shoe industry has been well known even beyond the island's shores ever since the late 19th century. Locally made shoes can be bought in numerous outlets in the city centre as well as on the outskirts (towards Maó and Cala en Bosc).

Below: weekly market
Bottom: Bastió de Sa Font

THE FESTA DE SANT JOAN

The Festa de Sant Joan, which takes place each year on 23–24 June, is celebrated all over Spain, but nowhere with such raucous abandon as in Ciutadella. On the previous Sunday, a live ram is carried around the town on the shoulders of a man dressed in sheepskins, representing John the Baptist. Then, for two days, the citizens of Ciutadella go wild, with crowds of people thronging into Plaça d'es Born and neighbouring streets to witness horseback processions, firework displays and jousting tournaments.

Most of the rituals enacted here revolve around the Menorcan passion for horses, and the *caixers*, or horsemen, who represent the medieval social classes, ride among the crowds, prancing and circling on their horses' hind legs. The longer a horse manages to stay on two legs, the greater the roaring appreciation of the crowd, which surges

Map
on page
36

Exploring on foot
The best way to explore Ciutadella is to walk, with an accurate map but no fixed route, at different times of the day and night. Inevitably you keep returning to the streets around the cathedral. At night, history comes alive here, with small architectural details – sundials, saints in niches, coats of arms – spotlighted by old-fashioned street lamps. By this time the fish restaurants beside the port are starting to fill up, but if you walk back along the creek and look up at the old wall, you can imagine past centuries, when the gates were locked from sunset to sunrise.

Veteran of the times

forward, trying to get as close as possible to the action. It may look as though some of the braver revellers are in imminent danger of being trampled underfoot, but the horses are light footed and very well trained. Daredevil antics also apply to the jousting, where the idea is for the rider to spear a hoop hanging from a wire in the middle of the square. The expectant crowd first closes in on the horse and rider, only parting at the last minute as they gallop at full speed towards the hoop, and then closing ranks again once they have passed. A successfully speared hoop is met with another roar of appreciation.

When night falls, the horses and riders have another task to perform: they trot around town calling in at people's homes and receiving a welcoming drink, an activity that is said to bring luck to the hospitable household.

CENTRAL SIGHTS

There is always something rather seductive about harbour towns, and this is definitely true of ★★ **Es Port ❶**, Ciutadella's harbour. The long narrow bay to which the British decided not to entrust their ships is utterly Mediterranean in character. The quays are almost overflowing with the chairs on the café terraces and bars, which have names like El Bribón or Es Moll. Skippers of all nationalities meet up here each evening for a few *copas* and *tapas* while their white yachts are lined up nearby, easily outnumbering the fishing boats.

Glass-bottomed boats wait to take passengers for extended trips along the coast. Local fishermen can be seen sitting outside the cafés from early morning onwards. The attractive backdrop to this scene is provided by the ochre-coloured town wall, with the fortified former Town Hall rising above it.

Go west along Camí de Baix, beside the harbour, then climb steps to Passeig de Sant Nicolau, and you will come to the **Castell de Sant Nicolau**, a 17th-century octagonal tower that once protected the harbour. Today it contains a museum (Tues–Sat 11am–1pm, 6–8pm; free) with old pho-

tographs and engravings. A bust outside commemorates David Glasgow Farragut (1801–70),
the son of a captain from Ciutadella, who fought
in the American Civil War and then conquered
New Orleans and rose to become the first four-
star admiral of the United States. When he visited
his father's town in 1867, he was given a hero's
welcome, with huge crowds lining the streets.

Star Attractions
• **Es Port**
• **Plaça d'es Born**

PLAÇA D'ES BORN

At the other end of the harbour the steps of Baix-
ada Capllonc, lead past souvenir stands and boutiques to the ★★ **Plaça d'es Born ❷**, the beating
heart of the town, and the scene every June of
the Festa de Sant Joan *(see page 37)*. This pretty
square is bordered by the former Town Hall and
the finest *palazzi* in Ciutadella, and looks lovely
at night when illuminated by the soft light from
the wrought-iron street lamps.

In the middle of the square, around the obelisk
commemorating those who fell in the Ottoman
attack of 1558, a lively market is held every Friday and Saturday selling textiles, jewellery and
Far Eastern items. From the **Bastió des Port**, the
northern side of the square, there's a magnificent panoramic view of the harbour. Next door
is the Cercle Artístic; the art association was
founded in 1881 but now it's just a café, a good

Below: Plaça d'es Born
Bottom: Ciutadella harbour

Map
on page
36

Hallowed hall
The neo-Gothic council hall inside the Ajuntament has several familial coats of arms on its wooden ceiling as well as portraits of illustrious Menorcans around the walls. You will probably only be able to see it on 9 July every year an account of the terrible attack on the city in 1558 by the Turks is read aloud in the hall.

place to mix with local people or simply sit back in a soft leather chair and enjoy a cup of coffee. The adjacent **Teatre Municipal d'es Born** shows films, and plays are performed here, too.

The imposing building with high battlements that dominates the western end of the plaça is still known as the **Ajuntament** (Town Hall), although it is now the police headquarters. There was once a Moorish castle on this site, then a fortress, constructed by Alfonso III in the 13th century. Today's building, which dates from the 19th century, has a colourful floor mosaic in front of the main entrance showing the municipal coat of arms, in which the blue of the Mediterranean and the grey-brown of several impregnable-looking battlements predominate.

GRAND PALACES

The magnificence of the opposite side of the square is hard to beat: from right to left stand the **palaces** of the Saura, Salort and Vivó families, with their richly decorated façades. Time is taking its toll, however. The ground floors contain cafés and souvenir shops, and a Burger King outlet is vying for custom with the specialities of Menorcan cuisine. As the descendants of the noble families now live in Barcelona or Madrid and only make brief visits during the summer, the

Saura Palace

shutters on the upper storeys are usually closed.

The **Palau de Torresaura**, with its two wings, has a mighty portal with a coat of arms set into it, a magnificent inner courtyard, fine loggias and even Renaissance-style *putti* on the roof. The only one of the palaces that can be visited is the splendid **Palau de Salort** ❸ (May–Oct, Mon–Sat 10am–2pm), built in 1813, with one of its side wings facing the square, and the entrance at the side in Carrer Major del Born. You can visit the ballroom and a mirror hall, the dining room, an historic tiled kitchen and the children's bedroom, complete with cradle and pram. Alongside antique furniture, numerous paintings and family portraits, as well as several valuable tapestries, there is also a fine Buick dating from the 1920s.

The noble façade of the **Palau Vivó** is decorated by oriel windows and balconies and the atrium contains a magnificent double staircase, but unfortunately it is closed to visitors.

SANTA MARIA CATHEDRAL

The Carrer Major del Born leads between the *palazzi* – note the finely worked door-knockers with sea serpents and women's heads – to the **Plaça de la Catedral**, where a helpful tourist office is located and entertainers keep the crowds amused. The most prominent structure in this square, and the most important religious building in Menorca, is the single-aisled, square-cut ★★ **Catedral de Santa Maria** ❹ (daily 9am–1pm, 6.30–9pm; free). Begun around 1300, after the Moors had been driven from the island, it was built on the site of an earlier mosque, as were so many churches on the islands. Its bell-tower was once a minaret, and *marés* – the porous sandstone of Menorca – gives the cathedral its warm, golden-brown colour.

When the Turks invaded the town in 1558 they destroyed the original building. In 1795, after a great deal of intensive repair work, the church was elevated to the status of a cathedral when a papal edict gave Ciutadella a bishop. The façade is dominated by the neo-classical main portal, which dates from 1814. The original Port de la Llum,

Star Attraction
•**Catedral de Santa Maria**

Below: Saura Palace detail
Bottom: the cathedral

Map
on page
36

or door of light, from the 14th century, is decorated with a relief showing magnificent, fabled creatures and the coat of arms of Aragón and Ciutadella. The first thing you will notice when you go inside is the warm light falling through the colourful stained-glass windows. The 12 side chapels are also striking: most of them date from the Renaissance era, as does the Catalan Gothic main altar. The rather plain-looking but melodious organ was consecrated in 1993 in the presence of the present Spanish king, Juan Carlos I. Organ concerts, for which there is a small charge, are held daily at 11.30am in summer.

Below: Palau de Olivar
Bottom: detail from
Església del Roser

EPISCOPAL DELIGHTS

Opposite the main portal of the Cathedral is the neo-classical Palau de Olivar, which, like so many other *palazzi* in Ciutadella, is not open to visitors. At the 18th-century **Palau Episcopal** (Episcopal Palace) ❺ in the Carrer de Ca'l Bisbe there is a quiet inner courtyard that can be visited (Mon–Sat 9am–noon; free) and which connects the palace and the Cathedral. There is a fine view of the bell-tower, and benches in the garden on which to sit and relax.

The loggia-like entrance to the palace is Italian-influenced, and a tile picture on the Cathedral wall shows the *Madonna of Monte Toro*. Local people used to collect water from the well here, which now has a grille over the top and no longer contains any water.

In the Carrer Sant Sebastià, a few steps further on, the golden stucco work on the **Palau de Squella** ❻ glints in the sunshine. In 1867 this is where Admiral David Glasgow Farragut, hero of the American War of Independence and son of an emigrant from Ciutadella, stayed when he visited the island in 1867 *(see page 39)*.

Opposite the Porta de la Llum, the Cathedral's south door, narrow Carrer del Roser branches off, leading towards **Es Roser** ❼ (Mon–Sat 10am–1pm, 5–8pm; free), which dates from the 17th and 18th centuries. Its beautiful doorway is adorned with flower, fruit and leaf ornamentation. The church has been deconsecrated and restored and the **Sala Municipal d'Exposicions** hosts exhibitions of contemporary art.

TWO PALACES

A few metres further on, in Carrer Santíssim, is the ★ **Palau Saura** ❽ (Mon–Sat 10am–1pm, 6–9pm; free), another townhouse owned by the once influential Saura family. The *palazzo*, which took just one year to build in 1697, has recently been restored. The clear lines of the façade, the windows and the projecting roof reveal the feeling for form and the craftsmanship of the island's master architects of that era. Inside, there is an impressive staircase and several Roman amphorae to admire.

The **Palau Martorell** ❾ directly opposite is every bit as attractive, but is closed to the public. Locally, this 17th-century building is referred to merely as the *Cas Duc*, or Duke's House; the exterior has striking semi-circular balconies and deep-set windows.

A VISIT TO THE MARKET

Turning right takes you to Carrer del Castell Rupit. Things get noisy and busy again at the street's end, on the arcaded Plaça de la Llibertat, and there are some fascinating aromas in the air.

Below: local advert
Bottom: C'al Bisbe

Map on page 36

In the morning (Tues–Sat) the ★★ **Mercat** ❿ is held here. The small 19th-century pavilion is filled with stands of seafood and fish, and beyond the wide-open doors of the green-and-white-tiled market hall opposite there are mountains of meat and sausage for sale.

Around the market are numerous bars, like the Piscolabis or the Ulises, where the clientele is almost always entirely local. Some of the older customers live in the retired people's centre in the nearby Carrer de l'Hospital de Santa Magdalena, conveniently set right in the middle of town with life going on all around it.

Below: fish in the market
Bottom: exploring the backstreets

In the Casa de Cultura opposite, young men and women can be seen walking to and fro from the music school with heavy instrument cases; there is also a well-stocked town library here (the books are mainly in Spanish but there are also sections with English, French and German titles).

CARRER DES SEMINARI

Retrace your steps a short way to the **Carrer des Seminari** ⓫, a street that is a cultural and historical monument. The **Convent i Església del Socors**, was once part of an Augustinian monastery destroyed by the Turks and rebuilt in the 17th century. The twin-towered Renaissance church was begun in 1648. Today it serves as the auditorium for the music conservatory of the Capilla Davidica, so it is not open to the public except on special occasions when concerts are held in the **Seminar Concilar** – the only opportunity to study the rather damaged but still fine ceiling frescoes.

There is a soaring cloister and a pretty monastery garden with lemon trees and a well, which was laid out between 1616 and 1676, and restored in the 1990s. The hallowed halls contain a seminary, and there is also a library here, together with the small **Museu Diocesà** (Diocesan Museum; May–Oct, Tues–Sat 10.30am–1.30pm; entrance charge), which not only has a large collection of prehistoric archaeological finds and ecclesiastical artefacts but also some landscape paintings by the Catalan artist Pere Daura (1896–1976), who was born in Ciutadella.

On the next corner is another property that once belonged to the Saura family: the **Can Saura** was built by an 18th-century British governor for Joan Miquel Saura, who took the Habsburg side against the Bourbons in the War of the Spanish Succession and forfeited his house as a result. The ground floor is occupied by a branch of the Caixa de Catalunya savings bank, which is funding extensive restoration work.

COMMERCE AND CHRISTIANITY

There are several appealing little boutiques to discover on the other side of the street, selling handmade bags, lampshades and Malayan sarongs. Alternatively you could try an *horchata* – a sweet milky drink made from ground almonds – at the Café Paradis, while admiring the portal of the monastery.

On the corner of Carrer del Sant Christ is the tiny **Església del Sant Christ** (daily 9am–1pm, 5–9pm; free) which dates back to 1667. The church contains an unusual and powerful crucifixion, the *Christ dels Peraires*. It is highly treasured because, in the 17th century, beads of perspiration are said to have appeared on Christ's face.

Star Attraction
• Mercat

Eye for detail
When you visit the Diocesan Museum, be sure to take a look at the neo-classical door in the boundary wall. It is crowned by an odd sculpture of the Virgin Mary, threatening a dragon-devil with a hammer and cudgel.

Seminar Concilar ceiling

Map
on page
36

Below: Crucifixion, Sant Christ
Bottom: Municipal Museum

UNDERNEATH THE ARCHES

On the triangular Plaça Vella, a column with the
flag of the Knights of St John commemorates Ciutadella's famous festival, the Festes de Sant Joan
(see page 37). There is also a plaque here commemorating the birthplace of Josep Maria
Quadrado (1819–96). He lived in Mallorca in
his later life and became famous as a novelist and
historian who spoke out strongly in favour of
Catalan as a literary language.

Off the tiny square, with café tables out in the
centre, runs a narow street officially named after
Quadrado but always known as ★★ **Ses Voltes**
(The Arches) ⓬. There are deep Gothic-style
arcades in the white buildings on either side where
you can window-shop or just enjoy the cool shade
on a hot day.

Some marvellous tourist-oriented shops include
confiterias (sweet shops), *pastellerias* (pastry
shops) selling huge, gift-wrapped *ensaimadas*
(see page 106), and fashion and shoe shops. This
is a spot you can fall in love with very quickly.

THE MUNICIPAL MUSEUM

From here, you could make a detour along the
Carrer de Santa Clara, a street full of jewellery
shops, to the town's fortifications. This area is the
oldest in Ciutadella. The Palau de Lluriac, with
its pillared windows, was formerly yet another
property of the Salort family and today houses the
offices of the island's main newspaper, although
the adjoining 17th-century Convent de Santa
Clara is still inhabited by nuns.

At the end of the street, the stocky-looking
★ **Bastió de sa Font** ⓭ was built between 1677
and 1692 and is part of the few remains of Ciutadella's former fortifications. The excellent
Museu Municipal (Mar–Sept, Tues–Sat
10am–2pm; entrance charge) is housed here and
its numerous vaulted rooms contain a rich collection of archaeological finds from all epoch's
of the island's history, as well as interesting mod-
els of megalithic villages. A vaulted antechamber is sometimes used for art exhibitions.

PLAÇA NOVA

On the way back towards the centre, you could go along Carrer de Sa Muradela, overlooking a dry river bed and turn left, just before Plaça des Born, to visit the **Casa-Museu del Pintor Torrent** (May–Oct, daily 11am–1pm, 7.30–9.30pm) devoted to the work of the painter born in Ciutadella in 1904, who has been called 'the Menorcan Van Gogh'.

Alternatively, retrace your steps to Ses Voltes, then on to ★ **Plaça Nova** . This is where the people of Ciutadella like to gather; you could join them by taking a seat outside the Café Xoriguer or Cafeteria Al Arco, to watch the world go by.

If you have time and energy stroll along the pedestrianised Camí de Maó and look at the houses and shops with their beautiful wrought-iron balconies. At the eastern end, in the noisy **Plaça de Alfons III** , known locally as the **Plaça de Ses Palmeres** (Square of the Palm Trees), you will see people feeding swarms of ever-hungry pigeons.

On the far side of the square, across a busy main road, the **Museu Molí des Comtes** (Jun–Sept, Tues–Sun 10am–1pm), housed in an attractive white, 18th-century windmill, displays machinery and other milling artefacts. Adjoining it, the Centre de Artesania holds a few shops but seems decidedly half-hearted and under-used.

Star Attraction
• Ses Voltes

Cranial surgery
Some of the ancient skulls on view in the Museu Municipal show wounds caused by trepanning in cranial surgery, which indicate that the *talyotic* culture must have developed advanced surgical techniques. In some cases the wounds have healed over, proving, somewhat remarkably, that the patients must have survived.

Plaça Nova

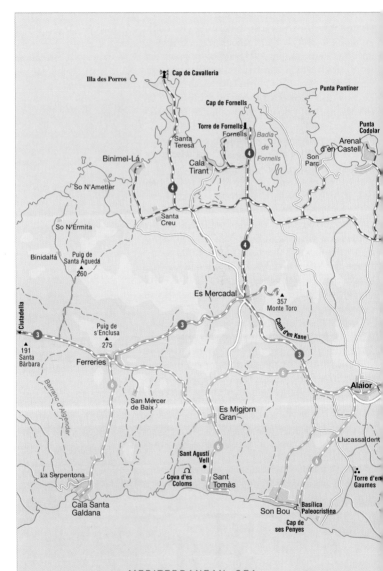

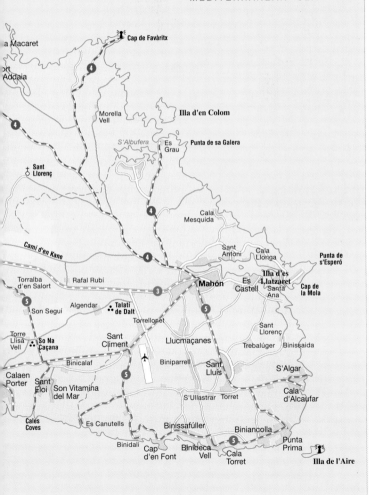

ROUTES 3 - 6

0   3 km

MEDITERRANEAN SEA

a Macaret

ort
Addaia

Cap de Favàritx

Morella
Vell

Illa d'en Colom

S'Albufera   Es
Grau   Punta de sa Galera

Sant
Llorenç

Cala
Mesquida

Camí d'en Kane   Sant
Antoni   Cala
Llonga   Punta de
s'Esperó

Torralba
d'en Salort   Rafal Rubí   Mahón   Es
Castell   Illa d'es
Llatzaret
Santa
Ana   Cap de
la Mola

Son Seguí   Algendar   Talatí
de Dalt

Torrellonet

Torre
Llisá
Vell   So Na
Caçana   Sant
Climent   Llucmaçanes   Sant
Llorenç

Trebalúger   Binissaida

Binicalaf   Biniparrell   Sant
Lluís   S'Algar

Calaen
Porter   Sant
Eloi   Son Vitamina
del Mar   S'Ullastrar   Torret   Cala
d'Alcaufar

Cales
Coves   Es Canutells   Binissafúller   Biniancolla

Binidali   Cap
d'en Font   Binibeca
Vell   Cala
Torret   Punta
Prima   Illa de l'Aire

Map on pages 48–9

Camí d'en Kane

If you have time, it's well worth getting to know the 16km (10 miles) or so that still survive of this old route across Menorca. The narrow, bendy road leads past *parets seques*, those dry walls so typical of the island, remote farms, rich green meadows or oak groves. Sometimes ancient pine trees form avenues.

The Camí d'en Kane starts on the Maó–Fornells road at Km3.6, rounds the cemetery outside Alaior, and comes out onto the C721 just before Es Mercadal. A further 4-km (2-mile) section can be found northwest of the town in the direction of Ferreries, but it ends in tracks and eventually at the main road again.

Cycling the Camí d'en Kane

3: Along the Island Axis

Maó – Alaior – Es Mercadal – Monte Toro – Puig de Santa Agueda – Naveta d'es Tudons – Ciutadella (88km/54 miles)

The road from Maó to Ciutadella runs 45km (28 miles) along the backbone of Menorca. Other roads branch off it to coves, beaches, villages and the tourist resorts. Some are well-paved and well-marked, some are bumpy, narrow, and full of recently filled potholes, while others might be easy-to-miss tracks leading to prehistoric sites, fields of scrub or country estates. You will have to keep returning to this road to get around the island, because instead of a coast road, Menorca merely has an old horse track, the Camí de Cavalls *(see page 11)*.

JOURNEY OF DISCOVERY

Towns to discover to the right and left of the main Menorcan highway include Alaior, Es Mercadal and Ferreries, all of which have grown very slowly since the 14th century. All have parish churches, narrow streets and pretty squares with cafés and restaurants. There are also the ancient Talatí de Dalt, the Navetes de Rafal Rubi, the Naveta d'es Tudons and the Taula Torre Trencada, all built during an unparalleled period of construction some 3,500 years ago. Finally, the quiet charm of Menorca can best be appreciated during the early morning or early evening hours from the top of Monte Toro (357m/1,170ft), the highest 'mountain' on the island, with breathtaking all-round panoramic view.

LEAVING MAO

Leave Maó on the C721, the main road across the island, in a westerly direction and you will first find yourself travelling through the large commercial area of the capital. Yachts, motorboats and diving gear are on sale here, and there are outlets selling Spanish wines or glazed ceramics in every imaginable colour. Just beyond the point where the road branches away to the airport a small road leads off to the left, to two attractions.

The ★ **Sansuguet Estate** is where the Menorcan-born painter Francisco Sans Huguet set up a magnificent refuge for himself in 1926, after years of wandering through Europe and holding exhibitions in many of the great museums of Paris, Madrid and Toledo. Visitors are only allowed in if a member of his family is present, and visits cannot be planned. If you are lucky in your timing, there may also be a glass of red straight from the barrel, and the afternoon may become a long one. The paintings and drawings all around the house are signed with the artist's pseudonym 'Sansuguet', and alongside still-lifes and portraits and accurately rendered scenes from Paris or Toledo, there are a large number of Menorcan landscapes.

Below: Sansuguet Estate
Bottom: Navetes de Rafal Rubí

TALATI DE DALT

One of Huguet's frequently recurring motifs, the megalithic settlement of **Talatí de Dalt** (daily 10am–sunset; entrance charge in summer), is just a stone's throw away, surrounded by gnarled mastic trees, olives and carobs. It was inhabited until Roman times, and is considered to be one of the better-preserved ancient sites of Menorca. Stone steps lead over a wall into the village, which, with

Map
on pages
48–9

its *taula* and *talayot*, weathered circle of stones and caves, still gives visitors a very good impression of a prehistoric settlement. The *taula* is enclosed in a circular plot of land. A stone column leans against it, seeming to support the table-shaped structure.

From the high *talayot* there is a fine view of the surrounding area, and of the maze of stone walls across the island. The present and the past sit side by side: nearby, the Talayot Torelló is visible, and at the airport charter planes can be seen landing and taking off. If you happen to be visiting Menorca in the springtime, there will be wild flowers blooming everywhere: red poppies, mauve, yellow and white crocuses and knee-high thistles with purple flowers.

Below: Talatí de Dalt
Bottom: pointing the way

MEGALITHIC STRUCTURES

Since there are roughly two prehistoric sites per square kilometre on this island, you'll make very slow headway if you want to visit each one. Just 1.5km (1 mile) further on you can leave the main road again and visit the *talayots* of **Binaiet Vell** on a small rise to the right, plus the prehistoric site of **Sant Vicent d'Acaidús**. The highlights of this village are two *circuli* – buildings on a circular ground-plan that were used as living accommodation 2,500 years ago.

The ★★**Navetes de Rafal Rubí** (open site; free) can be found in a field to the right of the road. These megalithic structures, formerly family tombs, resemble overturned boats. Archaeological finds here have dated their origin to around 1500BC. A narrow track that also leads to the parallel Camí d'en Kane *(see page 50)* will take you to a rickety wooden gate, leading to a field and to the first and best-preserved of the *navetas*. If you crawl inside the low doorway you will see the antechamber and several more rooms. Light penetrates through several cracks, and also through the larger *naveta* nearby. Using the simplest of means, the stones were carefully placed side by side here – and so densely that not even a hand can fit through the cracks.

navetes d'enterrament **ACCES**
de Rafal Rubí →

ALAIOR

Next comes the third-largest town on Menorca and also its cheesemaking centre: ★★ **Alaior** (pop. 6,400). Most of the cheese known as *Queso de Mahón* and marketed in the capital is actually made here. Whole cheeses or sections can be bought from wholesalers or at cooperatives such as Coinga or Quesos Torralba, or from the small shop opposite the La Payesa factory (past Plaça de Sant Francesc). The factory itself cannot be visited, but it can be smelled as you approach.

This pretty town has other attractions besides its cheese, however. To get a good view of unwelcome guests, it was built on a hilltop. The narrow streets and house façades are definitely worth a closer look; with its colourful houses and window frames, Alaior comes across as generally far more colourful than other towns on Menorca.

GEM OF A COURTYARD

One gem is the ★ **Plaça de Sant Francesc**, a courtyard surrounded by four-storey buildings (now private residences) that once belonged to the neighbouring Franciscan Convent de Sant Diego. Its inhabitants refer to it poetically as *Pati de Sa Lluna* (Courtyard of the Moon). With fine galleries, a well and dangling potted plants, this courtyard has a wonderfully light atmosphere that

Star Attractions
• Alaior
Navetes de Rafal Rubí

Below: local cheese
Bottom: Alaior

Map
on pages
48–9

counteracts the severity of its geometrical architecture. The Convent de Sant Diego itself is now a **Centre Cultural** (Wed–Fri 10am–1pm, 6–9pm, Tues 6–9pm, Sat 10am–1pm; free) which holds exhibitions with artesan and rural themes.

The church of **Santa Eulalia**, which dominates the town, has a plain sandstone exterior and the decoration inside is also very restrained. At the end of the 17th century this massive church replaced a previous structure, built when the town was founded by Jaume II in the 14th century.

REPRESENTATIVE BUILDINGS

In the narrow Carrer Major, the **Can Salort** is highly reminiscent of one of the feudal *palazzi* of Ciutadella. Obviously the people of Alaior weren't inclined to leave all the representative buildings to the island's former capital.

Opposite is the **Casa Consistorial**, which is another name for Ajuntament (Town Hall). Built in 1612, later than the town halls of Ciutadella and Maó, it is the finest on the island. The façade has an elaborately decorated balcony and even more decorative flags.

Take a look through the main door, where you'll see a magnificent flight of stairs and an elegant patio. There is also a collection of paintings centred on regional historical events. One real highlight is the Gothic *Rei Jaume II de Mallorca* by Miguel Alejandre, which you will be able to see if you attend one of the art exhibitions that are sometimes held on the first floor.

CEMETERY

While in Alaior you could visit the ★★ **cemetery**, situated 1.5km (1 mile) north of the town. Cemeteries are not everyone's idea of a tourist site, of course, but the niche graves set close together, monumental tombs and well-tended white funerary chapels are quite splendid.

On the way to the cemetery you can also look at the road known as Es Cós, which was used as a racecourse during British rule here. It is lined to

Two views of Alaior cemetery

right and left by white-painted benches where spectators used to sit. The grandstand can be made out just to the left of the cemetery. This was where the town worthies used to sit and a small flight of steps led up to it. The Camí d'en Kane *(see page 50)*, the old cross-island route used by the British, also leads past the cemetery.

Star Attraction
• **Alaior Cemetery**

DETOUR TO ERMITA DE SANT LLORENC

Since you are travelling eastwards there's a worthwhile detour at this point to the ★ **Ermita de Sant Llorenc de Binixems**. A bumpy track leads off to the left, passing remote farms and quarries to arrive at one of the oldest churches on the island. Its existence has been dated back to the early 14th century. After its destruction by an earthquake in 1654, it was rebuilt in the Renaissance style, but in 1898 it had become so dilapidated that it had to be renovated at great expense. And there it stands alone, surrounded by fields of grazing cows.

> **Festival time**
> The Ermita de Sant Llorenc is often closed, but things get very busy once a year during the festival of St Laurence, which takes place in mid-August. A procession of riders from Alaior comes to visit the church. The saint can be seen in a medallion above the main door.

ES MERCADAL

If you continue westwards along the main road now you'll reach the **Es Puig Mal**, or Mountain of Evil – so watch your driving. Here the road reaches its highest elevation of 200m (720ft), and

Es Mercadal from above

Map
on pages
48–9

Es Mercadal specialities
Most of the cooks in Es Mercadal specialise in Menorcan cuisine; the owner of the Ca n'Aguedet restaurant has even brought back viticulture to the island and is the exclusive provider of genuine Menorcan wine. The small almond macaroons known as *amargos* are also delicious. Es Mercadal is also famous for shoes: the *abarcas* (leather sandals whose soles were originally made of tyres) have been manufactured here for many years.

from now on Monte Toro, which provides the very best all-round view of the island, is constantly in sight until the town of ★ **Es Mercadal** (pop. 2,400) appears at its feet.

Brilliantly white houses contrast with the green of the surrounding landscape, giving this 700-year-old municipality its striking appearance. Es Mercadal's popularity derives not only from its central location as a starting-point for hikes across the Monte Toro region but also from the excellent food served here, which has a high reputation throughout the island *(see page 107)*.

HISTORIC CISTERN

The largely dry river bed of the Torrente makes it clear why one 18th-century structure is important to the people of Es Mercadal: the *aljub*. This cistern, 20m by 40m (65ft by 130ft) and 9m (30ft) deep, was built at the behest of English governor Richard Kane between 1736 and 1740. Kane had noticed the connection between the water shortage and the frequent diseases on the island, and financed the construction out of his own pocket. Today, the cistern is still opened on Saturday morning. That's when the local people take their buckets or canisters along and take a few litres of chlorine-free rain water home with them, after they have caught up with the latest gossip.

18th-century cistern, Es Mercadal

MONTE TORO

From now on the views get spectacular, along the well-maintained road, full of hairpin bends, that leads up to the ★★★ **Monte Toro** (357m/1,170ft), or along the hiking routes to the top. After a good hour's walk you will find yourself confronted by a stunning, all-round view from the top of Menorca's highest peak. It extends from the Cap de Cavalleria in the west to the beaches of the south coast – and on clear days you can even make out Mallorca in the distance without a problem. This sacred peak is crowned by a massive statue of Christ, next door to a forest of radio and television antennae. The statue is spreading his arms out to bless the Menorcans who fell during the Spanish wars in Morocco in the 1920s.

ANCIENT CENTRE OF PILGRIMAGE

There used to be a Gothic monastery on this peak. the Santuari de la Mare de Deu del Toro, which was the spiritual centre of the island. An Augustinian, baroque-style pilgrimage church replaced it in the 17th century, but it was desecrated in the Spanish Civil War and much of what you see today dates from the 1940s. There is a functioning convent here, too, and the remains of a defensive tower. This ensemble is linked by a picturesque, cloistered courtyard with a well, old ploughshares, stone benches and glossy plants. A sculpture group commemorates the priest Pedro Camps as well as the Menorcans who emigrated with him to North America in the 18th century, and founded the town of St Augustine.

The church and the convent are both consecrated to the Verge del Monte Toro, who is worshipped as the island's patron saint. According to the legend, a wild bull led a group of monks to a cave where they discovered a statue of the madonna. This statue, which was rescued in 1936, today adorns the altar in the church. Despite this story, the name actually derives from the Arab word *al-tor*, which means 'high place'.

Star Attraction
• **Monte Toro**

Below: Hermitage door, Monte Toro
Bottom: Fornells from Monte Toro

Map on pages 48–9

A NUN'S LIFE

It's hard to believe the nuns have time for the contemplative life, when one considers how amazingly busy this place is every day of the week. A souvenir shop and a restaurant help keep them above water financially. The shop contains everything that is even slightly souvenir-like, from a colouring book to a copy of the Christ statue, while the restaurant is a good place to sample *carquinyols* or *amargos* from Es Mercadal while enjoying the view across the Tramuntana and the Migjorn. During the summer this spot is only ever really quiet in the early morning or evening, when the hordes of visitors have disappeared.

Below: statue of Christ, Monte Toro
Bottom: Ferreries street

FERRERIES

The fifth-largest town on the island, **Ferreries** (pop. 3,700), is also the highest. It lies at 142m (465ft) above sea-level, but is far less picturesque than Alaior. Even though the town centre, with its narrow streets, its Plaça de l'Església and parish church of **Sant Bartomeu**, is attractive, the scene is dominated by a large area of new housing with high apartment blocks and an industrial area.

Founded by Jaume II of Mallorca at the beginning of the 14th century, Ferreries consisted of just a few houses and a village church until the 18th century, and was known mainly for its black-

smiths. After Governor Richard Kane decided to build the connecting road between Maó and Ciutadella the town prospered, and freed itself from dependence on Es Mercadal.

No-one is sure whether the name derives from *la fraria* (place of the monks) or *ferrería* (smithy), but the community today lives from a thriving furniture and shoe industry. The centre of action in Ferreries is the Plaça d'Espanya, where a large market is held every Saturday morning.

The best thing about Ferreries is that it makes a good starting-point for walks through the surrounding area. A variety of different landscapes converge here: the flat land in the west, the hilly north and the ravine-filled south. There is a small **Museu de la Natura** (May–Oct, Tues–Sat 10am–1pm, 6–9pm; entrance charge) in the town, which focuses on environmental issues.

PUIG DE SANTA AGUEDA

Just 3.5km (2 miles) outside Ferreries you will see a sign to the estate of **Binisues** on the right-hand side of the road. This is a stately home belonging to one of Ciutadella's noble families and is complete with the original furnishings. There is a museum of rural life here, as well as a pleasant restaurant with a big terrace, delicious wine and a great view.

There's another reason to come here: a walk to the summit of ★★ **Puig de Santa Agueda** (264m/866ft), the third-highest peak on the island; be sure to have good strong shoes or boots with you.

Leaving Binisues on your left, park your car at the old schoolhouse and take the footpath that leads up behind it to the right. The walk takes about half an hour; at first the steep path leads through a grove of cork oak and is difficult to negotiate because of rocks and stones. After 15 minutes or so, you will reach a remarkably well-preserved section of paved Roman path, evidence that the hill was already fortified in Roman times.

On the summit are the ruins of the **Castell de Santa Agueda**, an old Arab fort dating from the Moorish occupation. The governors of Medina

Star Attraction
• **Puig de Santa Agueda**

Below: church of Sant Bartomeu
Bottom: Ferreries

Map on pages 48–9

👁 **Ancient Quarry**
Close to Torre Trencada, on the old road from Ciutadella to Maó, S'Hostal is a disused limestone quarry that has been turned into an unusual open-air museum. Workmen give demonstrations of quarrying techniques and you can walk right down into the quarry, beaneath the sheer limestone walls. It was from quarries such as this that the stone for Naveta d'es Tudons was probably extracted.

Minurka had their summer palace here, and it was the final Muslim stronghold to surrender after the Christian invasion. You can also make out the foundation walls of a chapel to St Agatha, as well as the ruins of a farmhouse that was in use until the 19th century. But the real rewards for taking this hike are the incomparable silence, broken only by the odd bleat of sheep, the rich vegetation, and a view of Menorca that is second to none.

PREHISTORIC SITES

The prehistoric village of **Torrellafuda** was probably inhabited until Moorish times, and is hidden away to the left of the main road beneath holm oaks, amid knee-high thistles. There are several ancient stones lying around, and the *talayot* here is thought to be the largest on Menorca. A surrounding wall full of passageways, and several Roman tracks nearby prove that the settlement was once of great importance to this region.

Menorca's picture-postcard prehistoric site, the ★ **Taula Torre Trencada** (Apr–Oct, daily 8am–9pm; Nov–Mar, 8am–6pm; free) is only 1km (½ mile) away as the crow flies, but to reach it you have to go back to the C721, then turn left 2km (1 mile) further on (on the Camí Vell) and follow a bumpy asphalt track between high walls (keep left at the fork). The top stone of the *taula* is 3m (10ft) above the ground and supported by two other stones rather than just one – an unusual feature. The stone circle that belongs to it has survived the ravages of time, and there are several small funerary caves here too Although some of the stone slabs get used as picnic tables these days, the Torre Trencada is as captivating as ever.

Torre Lliafuda

NAVETA D'ES TUDONS

The fact that there is a route leading from the main road to the car park at the ★★★ **Naveta d'es Tudons** (open site; free) is significant, for this remarkable Bronze Age burial chamber standing in the middle of a field is the most famous prehistoric monument in Menorca. Since being excavated in the 1950s, it has become a magnet for visitors to the island, and is included on nearly all organised day trips from Mallorca.

During the excavations, the remains of 50 people were discovered in this two-storey *naveta*, with its distinctive boat-like outline. Some were stored in quicklime and furnished with funerary ornaments of bronze. Despite the many finds, experts are still uncertain about the exact date of these *navetas* (derived from *navis*, the Latin word for a ship); theories vary from 2000BC to 1000BC. Be that as it may, the Naveta d'es Tudons is believed to be the oldest roofed building in Europe.

If you creep inside through the waist-high opening, you will see the two chambers above each other, separated by a ceiling made of stone slabs. A well-beaten path leads to a small rise – the best place for photographing this mysterious site, which looks quite magnificent in the early morning or evening light.

CATTLE SHEDS

The stepped pyramids that you pass on the way to Ciutadella are not relics of prehistory, but far more recent. The inventive Menorcans used the numerous stones in their fields to build artistic-looking cattle sheds known as *barraques*, a common feature of the western hinterland.

Star Attraction
•**Naveta d'es Tudons**

Naveta d'es Tudons

Map
on pages
48–9

4: The North

Maó – Albufera d'es Grau – Es Grau – Cap de Favaritx – Port d'Addaia – Fornells – Cap de Cavalleria – Es Mercadal (115km/71 miles)

The Tramuntana, the barren northern part of Menorca, is a rough landscape characterised by sharp rocky outcrops and smooth hills. It is unspoilt and less touristy than the Migjorn in the south, although there are several modern tourist centres along its coast, such as Arenal d'en Castell. This region is good for hiking – and equally good for just stopping and staring.

The best of the scenery is along the coast: steep cliffs with lighthouses can be seen at Cap de Favaritx and Cap de Cavalleria. Between deep inlets there are protected sandy beaches and pretty little villages clinging to the slopes. The spiny lobster caught in Fornells is reputed to be the best in the western Mediterranean. If you want to hike, swim and eat superbly, plan to spend three days on this northern route.

Below: Albufera d'es Grau
Bottom: yachts and windsurfers at Es Grau

ALBUFERA D'ES GRAU

The second-largest wet biotope in the Balearic Islands, the ★★ **Parc Natural S'Albufera d'es Grau**, is located north of Maó. Follow the PM710 towards Fornells, and after about 2km (1 mile)

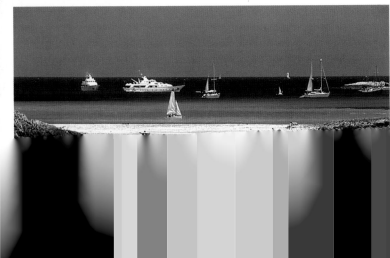

turn right along the PMV7102, with broad cycle tracks on either side, which twists its way through gently undulating landscape towards the coast for 10km (6 miles). In the 1970s, the biotope, centred on the only freshwater lake in Menorca, and home to lizards, turtles, and all kinds of migratory birds, was threatened by construction of a new, large-scale tourist development known as Shangri-La.

Protests from local people, from environmental groups and from the WWF brought the project to a standstill. Roads leading to nowhere and several remote houses stand today as reminders of the failed construction project. In May 1995, a year and a half after Menorca was designated a UNESCO-protected area, the island government declared the 1,800-ha (4,450-acre) area a nature reserve. A visitors' centre is under construction and may be completed by 2005. There are clearly-marked paths, which make it easy to find your way through the terrain, where olives, juniper and prickly pears give way to Aleppo pines and wiry marram grass as you approach the dunes.

Star Attraction
•Albufera d'es Grau

Birdwatchers' paradise
Cormorants, herons, fish eagles and other species now live on the shores of the S'Albufera d'es Grau lagoon undisturbed, while human beings are only allowed to make brief visits here. Bird-watchers can hike along marked routes. It's best to bring along insect repellent, however, and check for ticks when you get back to your hotel in the evening.

ES GRAU

On the eastern edge of the reserve is the small, attractive fishing village of ★ **Es Grau**, which was founded by people from Maó at the beginning of the 20th century. The white houses are huddled close together and tlocal people still outnumber visitors, even though Es Grau is definitely a tourist centre these days. There are several pleasant bars, and the long semi-circular bay with its fishing boats and yachts is a picture-postcard scene.

The sand on the beach is fine and the water calm – making this place ideal for children. A surfboard hire centre is not far away, and there are boat trips around the estuary and to the uninhabited **Illa d'en Colom** (Pigeon Island). The largest of Menorca's offshore islands, it has two beaches and several ruins. The remains of a quarantine station date back to British rule here.

Beyond Es Grau is a broad view of the jagged cliffs and the lighthouse at Cap de Favàritx (*see page 64*).

Es Grau beach

Map on pages 48–9

Below: Ermita de Fátima
Bottom: Port d'Addaia

PICNIC SPOT

Back on the PM710 to Fornells, the Camí d'en Kane *(see page 50)*, the old road between Maó and Ciutadella, branches off to the left. On the right of the PM710 you will see the **Ermita de Fátima** on a hilltop. There was a parish church on this site back in the Middle Ages, but today's structure dates from the 1950s. It's usually closed to visitors, but elderly people like sitting outside it at sunset and having picnic suppers.

CAP DE FAVÀRITX

After about 7km (4 miles) the recently resurfaced road to **★★ Cap de Favàritx** turns off to the right and runs through a barren, lunar landscape towards a headland lashed by the *Tramuntana* wind. This region supports next to no vegetation apart from scrub and violet-coloured succulents in spring. On stormy days, it is easy to imagine that the crumbling grey slate cliffs could collapse into the rough sea. That said, the cape has an eerie beauty.

At the end is the **Far de Favàritx**, the lighthouse, closed to visitors. Hardly any tourist buses make it as far as this remote corner of the island – usually just the odd angler or snorkeller. To the southeast, the two remote sandy beaches of **Cala Presili** and **Cala Tortuga** can be reached on foot from here in around half an hour.

PORT D'ADDAIA AND NA MACARET

Having returned from the cape, continue for around 1km (½ mile) along the PM710 to where an unmarked track leads off a bend to the right across fields to the **Ermita de Sant Llorenc de Binixems** *(see page 55)*. It can be reached from here on foot or by bike but not by car, because the route is too bumpy and the tree branches too low.

If you stay on the main road, however, and follow the signpost to Arenal d'en Castell, you come to **★ Port d'Addaia**, a pleasant enough place, although it does not have much character. The harbour lies at the end of a winding, fjord-like inlet that is best reached on foot. Villas, palm trees, ole-anders, an old defensive tower dating from the years of British rule, converted into a summer residence, all make Addaia seem like a big, well-ordered park. Little Port Llum is the local marina, usually filled with yachts.

The little harbour town of **Na Macaret** owes its foundation in the 19th century to islanders who enjoyed fishing here in the summer and turned this place into a home from home. The same applies today: people from nearby towns enjoy sitting on the terraces of summer homes during the evening, admiring their boats rocking on the waves. Once autumn comes, the shutters are closed, the boats are placed in dry dock, and Na Macaret falls back into its winter sleep.

ARENAL D'EN CASTELL

The next stop, **Arenal d'en Castell**, is one of the few places on the island to have succumbed wholeheartedly to mass tourism, complete with two ugly hotels towering over the beach and a dense complex of holiday apartments, supermarkets and other facilities. The beach – a wide arc of golden sand – is packed but perfect. Everything can be rented, from surfboards to umbrellas, yachts and beach chairs. In the evening life can get very noisy with all the discos and clubs.

Star Attraction
• **Cap de Favaritx**

Natural harbour
Chosen by the British as the bridgehead for their final invasion of Menorca in 1798, the natural harbour at Port d'Addaia is noted for its excellent anchorage for yachts. The boatyard at the marina specialises in complete refits.

The popular Arenal d'en Castell

Map
on pages
48–9

Travels on a donkey
For a leisurely ride through the Menorcan countryside, why not travel on a donkey? You can do this for a morning or afternoon from the Donkey Safari Park. Bear in mind, however, that the sacks used for saddles don't provide much of a cushion for bony backbones, and that the nags tend to go where they want rather than where you want them to go. Apart from the donkeys, there are lots of small animals for the children. There's also a small bar along with a café and shop, and the local people come here often to celebrate at the large barbecue sites, where they grill meat and eat it with *alioli*.

DONKEY RIDES AND GOLF

Back on the PM710, oak trees grow to the very edge of the road, which sometimes appears to cut straight through the rock. A Donkey Safari Park comes into view in the forest on the left *(see box)*.

To the north of the main road, in the luxury urbanisation of **Son Parc**, tourism comes into its own again, centred around a 9-hole **golf course**, the only place on Menorca where the sport can be played. The course is pleasantly situated among pine groves.

FORNELLS

★★ **Fornells** (pop. 650), reached via the resurfaced C-723, is an idyllically pretty little town, with most of the ingredients one likes to imagine in a Mediterranean port. Its narrow streets are lined with white, wooden-shuttered houses, there's a palm-fringed promenade along the calm lagoon, and colourful fishing boats bob side by side with yachts in the harbour basin. Visitors can hire surfboards and boats of all kinds, or get taken by a fisherman to visit the cavern known as the **Cova des Ingleses** (English Cove), the roof of which resembles the vault of a high church, with reddish-brown walls reflected in the azure water.

Fornells still has a working fishing fleet and is famous for its fish restaurants *(see page 108)*, one of the reasons the village is so popular with discerning people from Barcelona. King Juan Carlos and his family have been here on several occasions to eat *caldereta de llagosta*, a delicious, and expensive, lobster stew.

A patient donkey

FORTS AND BEACHES

You can walk or drive from the village to the **Torre de Fornells** (Tues–Sat 11am–2pm, 5–8pm, Sun 11am–2pm; free on Sun), built by the British on a desolate headland in 1802. The tower has recently been renovated and there's a small museum of local and military history inside. Below the tower, a little shrine, the Ermita de Loudres is surrounded by candles and flowers.

On the way there, at the water's edge, are the ruins of **Sant Antoni**, the 17th-century fortress that protected the little fishing village until it was destroyed by the Spanish in 1782.

To reach the the fine bay of **Cala Tirant** with its broad sandy beach,you can walk along a path that runs the length of the rocky coast, but it takes nearly four hours. Otherwise, you can drive along a bumpy track leading off the road to Cap de Cavalleria.

As you leave Fornells, heading for the cape, you will pass the elaborate entrance to the landscaped **Platjes de Fornells** 'country club', which you may have noticed on your way in. On the other side of the main road is **Ses Salines**, a small villa complex on an inlet, with a strip of beach, popular with keen sailors and windsurfers.

CAP DE CAVALLERIA

The region to the west of Fornells is known as Cavalleria, after the Cavalleries – the local estates built for military reasons after the *reconquista*. The whole area has been declared an area of special interest, not only because of the outstanding countryside, but because of the number of archaeological remains that have been discovered here. To the left and right of the road leading west there are fields of daisies and wild fennel. Any-

Star Attraction
• Fornells

Below: one of many fish restaurants
Bottom: Fornells harbour wall

Walk on the wild side

If you feel like getting more than just a fleeting impression of the rugged country in the north, leave your car near the Alairó farm and walk along one of the hiking paths westwards. There are a few olive groves, vegetable plots, and the odd farm – otherwise the region is characterised by wild vegetation and reddish-coloured rocks. At some point the north side of the Puig de Santa Agueda *(see page 59)* comes into view, and the paths keep on ending at closed gates bearing the message 'Propriedad Privada – Prohibido el Paso' so that in the end one has to obey them and set off back.

Feeding the goats

one interested in bird-life can make discoveries right at the roadside: birds of prey such as buzzards can be seen circling, and herons stalk the marshland. Soon the surface starts getting rough and stony and a dusty track leads northwards, just passing the fine sandy beach **Platja de Cavalleria** and the remote **Cala Mica** beach; if you feel like a swim at this point, keep left.

Further north still, you reach the little **Ecomuseu de Cap de Cavalleria** (open Mar–Jun and Oct, daily 10am–7pm; Jul–Sept, 10am–8pm; entrance charge), with displays on the history and ecology of the area, and finds from the Roman settlement of **Sanitja**, which has only recently been excavated. Archaeological digs are continuing and it is hoped more finds will be made. There's a pleasant little café with tables set out under the pine trees. The shallow bay near the Martello tower, the **Torre de Sanitja**, constructed by the British in 1798, was the third most important harbour on the island during Roman times. Today it just contains the odd fishing boat.

You can drive through the deserted landscape, past Sanitja to the ★★**Cap de Cavalleria**, Menorca's northernmost point. With a bit of luck, you may spot a rare type of vulture known as a *moixeta (Neophron percnopterus)*, en route. The steep coast reaches the imposing height of 89m (290ft), on the top of which is the **Far de Cavalleria**, protected from outsiders by a wall. All around it are caves dug during the Spanish Civil War, but today they are populated exclusively by lizards. It's best not to venture in too far because of the danger that they may collapse.

There's no alternative now but to go back along the same bumpy route. To the west is the beach of **Binimel-là**, an excellent place for a swim. In high season there's a *xiringuito*, or beach bar, that sells tapas. A path leads over hills, stone walls and sand dunes to **Cala Pregonda**, a pretty bay with a small beach that is hardly ever busy even in high summer. Hikers can venture even further to Cala Barril (three hours there and back); a long valley and a pine forest have to be crossed before the tiny bay comes into view behind a hillcrest.

5: The Southeast

Maó – Sant Lluís – Cala d'Alcaufar – Punta Prima – Binibeca Vell – Es Canutells – Cales Coves – Torralba d'en Salort – Alaior (69km/42 miles)

The southeast of Menorca has some attractive beaches, and sports centres make all kinds of watersports possible. The tourist settlements vary in quality: the colours and dimensions of the most recently built ones harmonise best with the landscape. Successful architectural design is seen in the unusual holiday village of Binibeca Vell, also known as Poblat de Pescadors (Fishermen's Village). Towns such as Sant Lluís are good places to go for lunch, followed by wandering and window-shopping.

ANCIENT SITES

The south of the island is also a good place for adventurers, however, as a glance at the *Mapa Arqueológico de Menorca* (available in local bookshops) will show: the region has a concentration of prehistoric sites, especially the *talayots* of Torrellonet and the major settlement of Torralba d'en Salort. In the Cales Coves – over 100 caves dug out of the rock – a 3,000-year-old culture can be examined *(see page 75)*. The Cova d'en Xoroi in the steep coastal rocks is quite dif-

Map on pages 48–9

Star Attraction
• Cap de Cavalleria

Below: a local shopkeeper
Bottom: Playa Punta Prima

Map
on pages
48–9

Watersports

For watersports along this flat, rocky coast the best address is the Club S'Algar Diving & Watersports. All kinds of sports are available, from windsurfing and sailing to water-skiing and jet-skiing – and divers are provided for too. Underwater caves, coral reefs and bays are visited during diving trips, and booking ahead in good time ensures a place on the boat.

ferent: a peaceful place by day, at night it becomes a cave disco, and the thumping bass tones resonate across the sea until the early hours. Plan roughly two and a half days for this route.

SANT LLUIS

Take the road from Maó to **Sant Lluís** (pop. 3,100), which is pleasant but unspectacular and has a couple of excellent restaurants: its narrow side-streets are grouped around the main Carrer de Sant Lluís. The park is as large as a football pitch and is filled with pine trees and climbing frames. In the **Centro Cultural** most of the older people tend to be engrossed in games of dominoes. The cups around the walls commemorate island football games.

Sant Lluís dates from the seven-year period of French occupation. They founded it in accordance with the vision of the French governor, with the streets arranged on a grid pattern. The plain white houses are dominated by the neoclassical **parish church** (1762), consecrated to the canonised Louis IX. The **Molí de Dalt** (Mon–Fri 10am–2pm, 6–8pm, Sat–Sun 11am–1pm; entrance charge), is a lovingly restored windmill housing a small folk museum with a collection of traditional farm implements.

Sant Lluís windmill

S'ALGAR

Take a left turn at the distinctive, dove-decorated roundabout on the edge of town, towards **S'Algar**, one of the first holiday resorts on Menorca. It gives one an idea of what most of the tourist areas in the south of the island are like: white, elegant apartments in long rows, broken up by palm trees and pines. Supermarkets here, car hire services there, plus a few restaurants and a discotheque – everything is catered for. Away from the water *(see box)* the days can be spent playing tennis, cricket, bowling, or horse-riding from the Club Hipic es Boeret.

A restored section of the coastal bridleway, Camí de Cavalls – which once ran around the entire Menorcan coast – connects S'Algar with Cala d'Alcaufar just to the south and onwards to the **Platja de Punta Prima** *(see below)*. It takes about two and a half hours there and back without a break, and remember that the sun beats down most of the time.

To the north of S'Algar a narrow footpath leads to the peaceful **Barranc de Rafalet**. Hikers should manage to get there and back in one and a half hours. After crossing a few fields and scaling several walls, the route descends into the valley and the fjord-like bay is reached at the end of an oak grove. The rocky outcrops here are often photographed to advertise Menorcan holidays.

*Punta Prima
shopping and beach*

CALA D'ALCAUFAR AND PUNTA PRIMA

A high embankment, a long bay and a little sandy beach are the special features of ★ **Cala d'Alcaufar**. The settlement has also retained something that other towns on the south coast lost long ago: the atmosphere of a fishing village. Low, white houses with wooden balconies and boat-houses with blue or green gates are the picturesque backdrop . While tourists lie on the beach, the fishermen mend their nets or paint their boats nearby.

One of the oldest holiday resorts on Menorca is **Punta Prima**, and it is highly regarded because

Map
on pages
48–9

Shipwrecks
The southernmost cape of Menorca around Punta Prima is not without its share of dangers, as can be inferred from the *Nautical Guide Menorca*, published in Maó: there are plenty of shipwrecks just under the waterline along this stretch of coast.

of its broad, sandy beach. As a result, the hotels and apartments do a busy trade in summer time, as do those who rent sunbeds by the water's edge. The outlets advertising surfboard hire have plenty of customers, too, and when the wind blows in from the sea there are numerous surfers out on the waves. Divers favour the coastline of the nearby **Illa de l'Aire**, with its tall lighthouse.

A String of Resorts

The section of coast to the west contains one *urbanización* after the next: Biniancolla is followed by Cala Torret, then Binibeca Vell, and finally Binissafúller and Binidalí. Most of these holiday complexes have features in common: one is the Arabic origin of the place names with the prefix *Bini*, which means 'property of the sons of...'. The other is the tiny beaches on sheltered bays, with just a few traces remaining of the fishing communities they once used to be.

The newly-built coast road, illuminated in the evenings by rows of modern street lamps, is ideal for making quick progress. Whenever it peters out, as it sometimes does, the best rule of thumb is to follow the one-way systems until another side-street heads towards the sea again – otherwise you may end up in a dead end in one of the interminable holiday complexes.

Imaginative architecture at Binibeca Vell

BINIBECA VELL

An exception to most of the holiday villages in this part of Menorca is ★★★ **Binibeca Vell** (also spelled Binibequer Vell). In 1972, when large high-rise hotels were being favoured in other areas, a tourist village, also known as Poblat de Pescadors, was built here in traditional Menorcan style. The plans were drawn up by the prize-winning Spanish architect, Antonio Sintes.

The houses, washed in brilliant white, look as if they are made of icing sugar. Stairs, chimneys and balconies are all completely harmonious. Narrow, winding alleys emerge into small interior courtyards, finished with natural stone and decorated with ceramic tiles; there are palms and orange trees at every corner, and bougainvillaea tumbles over garden walls. Bars and restaurants, a market place, a church and quay have also been constructed as an integral part of the settlement.

The overall effect is beautiful, but strangely unreal. There are few, if any, year-round residents, and the hordes of visitors dropped off by tour coaches during the summer months add to the impression that this is part of a film set.

ES CANUTELLS

Beyond Binidalí the coast road comes to an end, and another runs inland through beautiful landscape towards the centre of the island, past lush green fields, farms and a riding stable, until there's a left turn towards ★ **Es Canutells** and the sea again. This bay is beautiful, and surrounded protectively by rocks; the community here is small, as is the white sandy beach, and things remain calm and peaceful here in the summertime. Fishing boats filled with lobster pots dock at the quay, and elderly local people chat away outside their summer residences.

PREHISTORIC CAVES

The housing area of Ses Tanques is half an hour's walk to the east. Beneath it, along the imposingly steep coast, there are numerous ★ **prehistoric**

Star Attraction
• Binibeca Vell

Below: Binibeca Vell detail
Bottom: Es Canutells bay

Map
on pages
48–9

caves. Only try exploring them if you have a head for heights. Some caves contain several chambers and others have supports shoring them up – all have dizzying views of the sea below. The best view of all can be had from the rocky headland opposite, on which a British fort once stood.

SAN CLIMENT

The little village of **Sant Climent** is popular with residents of Maó. Peoplwho live in the 'Binis' stop at Carrer de Sant Jaume and buy all they need for the day, but don't spend much more time here. There's a little plaça and a parish church, a pub advertising 'Friday night knockout darts', a jazz club with good music and a *pastelería* with delicious *pastas* and *rosquillas* – and that just about sums up Sant Climent.

Below: Sant Climent jazz club holds jazz nights every Tuesday and Thursday
Bottom: Talayot de Torrellonet

TORRELONET

After all this indolent beach life, you shouldn't lose sight of the island's prehistory. There's a good detour to the northeast at this point to the highest surviving *talayot* on Menorca, the **Torrellonet**. As you open and close the numerous gates on the way there, you will hear charter jets taking off and landing nearby. The Torrellonet is the only *talayot* on the island which has a window, but

rather disrespectfully it has been equipped with flight tracking equipment for the airport. The steps leading up were worn away long ago – but there's a good view, as you would expect from a defensive tower.

If you continue along the path for around 500m (¼ mile), past a farm with some moody dogs, you'll catch sight of the **Basílica d'es Fornàs**. This early Christian church, built in the 5th or 6th century, is located above the foundations of a Roman villa. The remains of the three aisles and a filigree floor mosaic with peacocks, lions and foliage survive. The whole structure has been roofed over, and barbed wire protects it from unauthorised entry.

Along the road westwards to Sant Climent there are more, smaller *talayots* and also the excellent English-run Rancho Allenwood, which organises riding lessons as well as whole day rides with picnics included *(see page 110)*.

CALES COVES

Reaching the ★★**Cales Coves** (Cave Bays), requires some tough driving or an hour's hike from the Son Vitamina development, but it's worth the trip: the two bays with their high limestone walls and numerous prehistoric caves, several of which are on different levels, are among the most impressive sights along the south coast.

This double bay has been a popular harbour since antiquity. The first caves were dug here in around 1000BC, and by the 4th century AD there were around 100 of them. They were used later on as hiding places by pirates and fishermen, and today a small group of dropouts lives here.

In the summer time so many young backpackers are attracted here from all over Europe that hardly a free cave can be found. The municipal authorities in Alaior make regular attempts to evict people from this free accommodation, but the holes – which have been declared a Spanish national monument – are soon reoccupied, and adherents of natural living return to splash about in the picturesque bays.

Communal living
In Talyotic times, the caves of Cales Coves were used both as burial chambers and as dwellings, with the dead and the living housed in adjacent caves. The more modern caves, dating from the 4th century BC, are quite sophisticated in design, with windows, patios and separate cubicles for different family members.

The Cales Coves

Map on pages 48–9

Cova d'en Xoroi
According to legend this cave was once inhabited by a pirate named Xoroi, 'the one-eared'. He stole from the farmers in the region, eventually abducting a farmer's daughter and fathering three sons by her. His hiding place was discovered shortly afterwards, whereupon Xoroi jumped into the sea with his eldest son.

Below: Torralba d'en Salort
Bottom: Cova d'en Xoroi

CALA N' PORTER

Not far away, **Cala N'Porter** is tourist country again, and has a surfeit of apartments, restaurants, bars, discos, hotels, supermarkets and estate agencies eager to sell people second homes. The sandy beach can be reached from the village above by a long flight of steps cut into the surrounding limestone cliffs, by car, or by a little road train.

One highlight here is the ★ **Cova d'en Xoroi** (daily 11am–9.30pm; entrance charge) set into the steep cliffs. It is 25m (82ft) above the waterline, set between sea and sky. By day, you can explore the cave and sit in the terrace café to admire the scenery. At night, the cave becomes a disco and pop music thunders out until the early hours, accompanied by light shows.

TORRALBA D'EN SALORT

Along the road to Alaior with its many bends, are three prehistoric sites: first, on the left, are the almost-overgrown remains of the village of So Na Cacana, with two *talayots*. Another 800m (½ mile) further along the road you must turn left yet again to reach ★ **Torre Llisá Vell** (park at the first farm, then keep left and go past several walls). Its entrance area – an archway and walls 3m (10ft) thick – is the only intact one of a Menorcan *taula*.

The prehistoric settlement of ★★ **Torralba d'en Salort** (daily 10am–8pm, except first Sat in month; entrance charge) features remarkable building methods – the rocks were piled on top of each other long before the invention of the pulley. In around 900BC this settlement was one of the largest on Menorca, as can be seen from the imposing *taula*, two *talayots*, numerous ruined houses and caves. Two hearths were discovered near the *taula* during excavation work, and are thought to have served as altars for ritual animal sacrifices. A small bronze bull and fragments of a bronze figurine were also found, and they are now on display in the Museu de Menorca *(see page 29)*. A few years ago the Fundació de les Illes Baleares purchased the entire site, and it became the first archaeological park on the island.

6: The Rocky South

Alaior – Torre d'en Gaumés – Platja de Son Bou – Es Migjorn Gran – Cova d'es Coloms – Sant Agustí Vell – Cala Santa Galdana – Barranc d'Algendar (60km/37 miles)

The Migjorn, the southern central part of Menorca, is packed with ancient watchtowers and those massive stone tablets that make Menorca one enormous outdoor prehistoric museum. For some people the sites are places of pilgrimage, while others steer clear of them; some like meditating here while others see nothing but a meaningless heap of old rocks. The Menorcans swear that whoever touches a *taula* during the full moon will have good luck and true love for the rest of their life – so that's a good enough reason to visit a few of them.

WORLDS APART

The landscape in the south of Menorca is more gentle than that in the north, and there's more tourist development here too. The local inhabitants are said to be different as well – more warm and friendly than their northern compatriots. Near the sea there are pine groves and innumerable holiday apartment complexes. The powerful sunshine here in the south can get very hot at times,

Map on pages 48–9

Star Attraction
• Torralba d'en Salort

Son Bou beach is great for families

Map
on pages
48–9

Archaeological finds
Finds unearthed at Torre d'en Galmés include Phoenician ceramics and Roman coins as well as a bronze statue of the Egyptian god Imhotep.

providing a good excuse to seek shade during a day trip to the *barrancs* – deep gorges. The Barranc d'Algendar, for instance, has a sub-tropical climate and vegetation to match. This route should take two to three days to complete, and four if you go on the hikes as well.

TORRE D'EN GALMÉS

On the main road from Alaoir a well-surfaced track leads to the biggest megalithic settlement on Menorca, ★★ **Torre d'en Galmés** (Tues–Sun 10am–8pm; entrance charge except on Sun). It was discovered during the 1940s, but only properly excavated in the 1960s. More than 500 people are thought to have lived here, as long ago as 1000BC, and the settlement was probably the island's capital because it has three *talayots*, a temple area with a *taula*, long defensive walls, caves and cisterns. The oldest part of the site comprises the tomb chambers and a pillared hall covered by stone slabs – probably a place of assembly. A small road leads around the entire archaeological site, leading some visitors simply to peer at it from their car window. This town, inhabited until the Middle Ages by the Menorcans' forefathers, is like one enormous stone garden, full of flowers and lizards – and the view extends as far as Alaior and Monte Toro.

Torre d'en Galmés

CAP DE SE PENYES

Further on towards the coast, a narrow side-road, paved at first, leads to the 70-m (230-ft) high **Cap de se Penyes**. The best thing to do is park at the beginning of the route and continue on foot, so as to enjoy the view across the beach of Son Bou and the Basílica Paleocristina, with the Cap d'Artrutx far away in the distance. On its eastern side the cape is bordered by the jagged Barranc de Llucalari, one of the rough valleys in the south. To reach the fine sandy beach at the end of the *barranc* you should take one of the narrow paths further inland.

EARLY CHRISTIAN BASILICA

The remains of a 5th-century Early Christian structure, the **Basílica Paleocristina**, lie to the east of Son Bou, near the beach – which means that many of its visitors are clad in swimming trunks or bikinis. Its walls were discovered in 1951, and it is assumed that the basilica once formed part of a larger settlement, the streets of which can still be made out from aerial photographs of the surrounding area.

The basilica originally had three aisles, and seems to have been influenced by similar structures in North Africa. One highlight of the site is a monolithic font in the form of a clover leaf. In the nearby section of steep coastline, Menorcans of an even earlier age created a striking cave community. Several of their descendants have converted the caves into holiday residences.

PLATJA DE SON BOU

When you see the long, sandy **Platja de Son Bou**, sloping smoothly into the water, safe and perfect for children, it becomes clear why the adjoining residential developments of Son Bou and Torre Soli Nou, and the villa community of Sant Jaume, are grouped around it like a miniature amphitheatre. This panorama attracted the attention of tourism developers very early on. Several 11-storey hotel blocks date from the unplanned con-

Star Attraction
• Torre d'en Gaumés

Below: Son Bou basilica
Bottom: the beach

Map on pages 48–9

Arts and crafts
Art fans visiting Es Migjorn Gran can drop in at the Galeria Migjorn Graham Byfield in the Carrer San Llorec to admire and perhaps purchase the ceramics and watercolours produced by much-travelled English artist Graham Byfield, with motifs from all over the world, as well as the naïve paintings of Peri Rowan (May–Dec, Tues–Sat 10am–1pm and 6–9pm).

struction boom in the 1960s, but buildings are now limited to four storeys in height and no more development is permitted along the water's edge. Son Bou only comes to life in the holiday season – during the winter the area beyond the dunes is like one enormous ghost town. The beaches of Sant Tomàs *(see page 83)* almost join those of Son Bou, but that resort can only be reached by road from Es Migjorn Gran.

Between the dunes and the built-up part of the coastline is the largest area of marshland in the southern part of the island, **Es Prat de Son Bou**. It was thanks to the efforts of the environmentalist group, Grup Ornitológic Balear (GOB) that the marshland was not drained to produce more land for construction. The area has now been declared a nature reserve, and during a stroll through it you may be lucky enough to catch a glimpse of a kite, a falcon or similar species of bird.

ES MIGJORN GRAN

Hardly anything has changed in the small town of ★ **Es Migjorn Gran** since it was founded in the second half of the 18th century. It was the home of the doctor Francesc Camps, who was also an amateur archaeologist and Menorca expert; he documented numerous songs and local customs. The town's name changed from San Cristóbal to

Es Migjorn cemetery

Es Migjorn Gran when it became part of the municipality of Es Mercadal in 1990. Es Migjorn Gran means simply 'the big south'. The name San Cristóbal – which was given to the town and its 18th-century parish church by the Spanish – can still be seen on some maps of the island.

As the only one of Menorca's municipalities that does not lie on the main road, Es Migjorn Gran has a sleepy, provincial feel and lots of traditional rural architecture. The simple whitewashed houses along Carrer Major, none of which is more than two storeys, have balconies and wooden shutters, and some are decorated with blue tiles. The parish church of Sant Cristòfol, its square bell-tower topped by a cockerel, is satisfyingly proportioned. This little town has made a name for itself as a gourmet food centre over the past few years for its restaurants serving typical *cuina menorquina*, such as S'Engolidor or Migjorn *(see page 108)*.

BARRANC DE BINIGAUS

Not far from Es Migjorn Gran, several *barrancs* lead down to the sea. One of the strangest and wildest looking is the **Barranc de Binigaus**, which culminates at the beach of Binigaus to the west of Sant Tomàs. The hiking route there begins at the peaceful old cemetery, and passes three *talayots* as well as several fields full of pigs and cows. A path that is easy to miss (look for the red arrow on the wall) leads down into the narrow ravine, and alongside the usually dry river-bed below. Plants such as foxgloves flourish in the humid micro-climate on the valley floor, among liana-covered oak, almond and olive trees.

COVA D'ES COLOMS

If you look carefully on the opposite side of the ravine you will find the hidden entrance to the ★ **Cova d'es Coloms**, a cave known locally as 'the cathedral', and not without reason. Its dimensions are gigantic, although estimates of how big it actually is tend to vary wildly. Anyone who comes

Below: inside Es Migjorn church
Bottom: melon picking

Map on pages 48–9

here and tries to guess will soon realise that the rear section of the cave is concealed in the darkness. If you try to throw a stone at the ceiling, it won't get there (but may come back and hit someone on the head, so don't try it).

Excavations here have revealed numerous cult objects from pre-Christian times, when the ravines on the island were densely populated and the caves served as cult centres. Traces of campfires and graffiti on the walls are of a far more recent date, however. Young people like to have parties down here, dragging along generators for their amplifiers, guitars and microphones, as well as bringing all the necessary supplies of alcohol and food for barbecuing.

Below: Cova d'es Coloms
Bottom: a talayot

SANT AGUSTI VELL

At the entrance to the cave, an almost invisible stony path leads out of the ravine again. At the top on the right you will arrive at the prehistoric settlement of ★★ **Sant Agustí Vell**, which can also be reached by car if you park on the main road from Es Migjorn Gran to San Tomás opposite the Son Saura estate and then walk down.

The village's picturesque location at the steep entrance to the *barranc* makes it clear that even the earliest Menorcans knew the benefits of a good view. Visitors today like settling down for

picnics here, too. The settlement consists of the remains of temples, houses, walls, cisterns and storage chambers set in the rock, covered with stone slabs and known as *sitjots*. One of the two remarkably well-preserved *talayots* here can be entered. Once your eyes have grown accustomed to the darkness, you will see three supporting pillars and a kind of stone crossbeam holding up the ceiling.

SANT TOMÀS

Sant Tomàs, with a small collection of hotels and apartment complexes, is worth visiting for its splendid sandy beaches. They have been given a bit of artificial help in recent years, however: in 1989 a storm made off with all the sand and the white powder that crunches under your feet today had to be imported. They're packed of course, because families with children adore the place. The watersports provided are varied, and the beach bar of Es Bruc, with a large terrace facing the sea, is rather like an observation platform, providing a view of beach life from above.

SON MERCER

The journey from Es Migjorn Gran to Ferreries is like a roller-coaster ride. The road cuts deeply through the rock, leads past remote farms and attractive estates, and through green hills dotted with small fields of corn and potatoes. Almost 1km (½ mile) before Ferreries a rough track winding up the slope to the left is a good starting-point for a hike. Once you reach the top there's a good view of Ferreries, and if you follow the path further you'll reach one of the best views of the southern part of the island – the white limestone plateau and numerous hills and *barrancs*.

Roughly 600m (⅓ mile) beyond the farm of Son Mercer de Baix is the village of ★ **Son Mercer de Baix**, which tourists hardly ever reach. This is a pity, because the prehistoric settlement is one of the oldest on the island: people settled in this unique location on the edge of the Barranc de Trebaluger

Star Attraction
• Sant Agustí Vell

Peaceful alternative
If you prefer things a bit quieter than the bustle of Sant Tomás, take your sun-mat and walk along the 1.5-km (1-mile) path leading to the quieter beach of Binigaus, further to the west. If you walk westwards and stay close to the shore you'll also reach the beach of Son Bou around 40 minutes later.

Beach bar in Sant Tomàs

Map on pages 48–9

and the Barranc de Son Fideu around 4,000 years ago. Excavations have also revealed pottery shards dating from Phoenician and Roman times. The foundations of several houses resembling *navetas* have been discovered beneath olive trees, including the **Cova d'es Moro** (Moor's Cave), which is a listed monument. The cave is actually a well-preserved house with a roof supported by three stone pillars.

CALA SANTA GALDANA

Below: Cala Santa Galdana
Bottom: an alternative view

Another attractive route runs from Ferreries towards Menorca's most famous bay, the Cala Santa Galdana. Along the road, the **Club Escola Menorquina**, offers spectacular horse shows on summer evenings (Jun–Sept, Wed and Sun, 8.30pm; tel: 971 155 059), as does **Son Martorellet** (May–Oct, Tues and Thur 8.30pm and 10pm; tel: 609 049 493). The road then leads past Talaiot Binicalsitx and one of the two official campsites on the island *(see page 116)* before arriving at the bay of ★★ **Cala Santa Galdana**. For a superb view, walk to the end of the rocky promontory to the left of the road: rocks fall steeply down to the sea; islands and peninsulas can be seen offshore; and pine forests and ravines extend as far as the semi-circular beach.

QUEEN OF THE COVES

A perfect oyster-shell bay, Cala Santa Galdana, known as the 'queen of the coves', is one of the finest in the Balearic Islands. In the early 1960s it was overrun by mass tourism: there are three huge, high-rise hotels with room for 2,200 guests. The restaurants, bars, apartment villages and supermarkets arrived later, and in the summer the sandy beach is almost always full. Children splash about in the shallow water or race around in electric cars on a special track, while their parents laze under sunshades that stand in long lines. Surfing, sailing, snorkelling and diving are all provided. The astonishing thing is that, despite everything, the bay has managed to retain its beauty.

CALA MIGJORN AND CALA MACARELLA

To escape the summer crush, take a 20-minute walk, starting behind the Hotel Sol Gavilanes, through woodland, redolent with the smell of pines, to little **Cala Migjorn**, an idyllic cove with crystal-clear waters and huge caves. There are no facilities here, so bring supplies if you are coming for the day. It takes a little longer (30–40 minutes) to reach Cala Macarella and the smaller Cala Macarelleta to the west *(see page 88)*. Take the wooden steps from the back of a small car park beside the Hotel Audax, and follow a path through pine woods to these delightful bays.

Star Attraction
• Barranc d'Algendar

Wild orchids
Wild orchids are no rarity in the Barranc d'Algendar, and butterflies will be your permanent companion until dusk forces you to make your way back again.

BARRANC D'ALGENDAR

The ★★ **Barranc d'Algendar** runs from just outside Ferreries down to Cala Santa Galdana and shows you an unusual side of Menorca, especially in high summer. The colours are quite different, and a broad valley at the Santa Galdana end turns into a *barranc* and then a true ravine, with sheer, 80-m (260-ft) rocky walls. Close to the bay there are reeds on the banks of the river, and a scattering of wild fruit trees, but the narrower the ravine becomes, the more jungle-like the vegetation. There is a wealth of birdlife, too, including kestrels and kites. Organised hikes can be arranged in Cala Santa Galdana *(see page 109)*.

Snorkelling in the clear waters

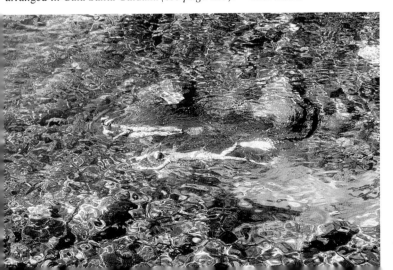

Map
on page
93

Map
on page
93

👁 **Sun, sea and sand**
Don't expect any architectural gems here – but as
recompense you'll get a broad range
of entertainment that starts at dawn
and goes on late into the night. The
prehistoric settlement of Son Catlar,
one of the largest and most interesting on the island, provides a respite
from sea and sand.

7: Beaches of the Southwest

**Ermita de Sant Joan de Missa – Cala en Turqueta
– Cala Macarella – Son Catlar – Son Saura –
Cala Santandría – Cap D'Artrutx – Ciutadella
(66km/41 miles)**

The dream beaches of Menorca are located to the
southeast of Ciutadella, and the locals refer to
them vividly as *platjes verges*, virgin beaches –
with white sand, azure water and picturesquely
framed by rocks. Shade is provided by pine
groves along the coast and the cave bars on some
beaches are like civilised additions. In this part of
the island, construction projects of all kind have
been successfully nipped in the bud. For instance,
protests from Menorcans in the early 1990s managed to stop Cala Macarella being turned into a
holiday enclave. The southwest coast, where the
beaches are no less attractive, is a different story
entirely: Cala Santandria or Cala Blanca are well-
established resorts, and construction work at Cap
d'Artrutx continues unabated.

If you want to indulge in lazy beach life and do
the hikes, it's best to allow two days for this route.

ERMITA DE SANT JOAN DE MISSA

Ermita de Sant Joan de Missa

Along the road to Cala en Turqueta there are signs
saying *Coto Privado de Caza* (private hunting
land) every few metres, starting from the Plaça
Jaume II in Ciutadella. Walls overgrown with
capers line the narrow road that leads to the bays
of the southwest; beyond them lie hidden gardens,
barren, stony fields and a few farms.

About 2km (1 mile) down a bumpy road from
the landmark Son Vivó farmhouse (an imposing
building with its name in large letters) is the
Ermita de Sant Joan de Missa (Mon 4–7pm; free)
a tiny chapel with battlements that was built in
1634. A previous building on the site was mentioned in records of 1330. From the square in front
there is a view of southwestern Menorca all the
way to the mountains of Mallorca in the distance.
As the chapel is usually closed, one way of making sure you gain access is to come on the Festes

de Sant Joan (23 June), when a procession of riders arrives here from Ciutadella. Beyond the chapel to the left, an easily missed country track branches off to the left and to the pine-lined Cala Macarella, but it's in poor condition. If you do want to go to this fine sandy beach and don't mind a rough drive and then an hour's walk, continue driving straight ahead and you can reach it via the old Camí de Cavalls.

Star Attraction
• Cala en Turqueta

MOTH TRAPS

Beyond the old country estate of Sant Francesc, a clay path leads down to the sea through a thick forest of oak and pine. Many of the pine trees have plastic boxes hanging from them – traps for tip moths which are renowned pine-tree killers throughout the Mediterranean. The females' propagation hormone emanates from the boxes, attracting the male moths, in an attempt to stop them from multiplying so rapidly. If nothing were done, just a few nests in one tree would be enough to destroy it in a few years' time.

Two views of
Cala en Turqueta

CALA EN TURQUETA

A right fork near Sant Joan de Missa leads to the lovely ★★ **Cala en Turqueta**. After a short way you come to another right turn, with a 'Welcome'

Map on page 93

Early warning
Watchtowers, such as the tower of Artrutx, were originally built to provide early warning of Ottoman fleets or pirate ships. Known as *atalayas*, they communicated with each other using light signals, and Monte Toro *(see page 56)* was the control centre.

sign and a caretaker who ensures that no more than 120 cars take the rough track down to the car park. You could walk down– it's only about 1 1/2 km (1 mile). This magnificent sandy beach and turquoise waters are perfect for families, and there are walks over the headland through pines and juniper bushes. If you are lucky, you may see a hoopoe or at least hear its call.There are few facilities at the beach but snacks, ice creams and cold drinks are on sale in summer.

High on a hill above the bay is the watchtower **Talaia d'Artrutx**, built in 1588. It is one of the best preserved of many such towers along the Menorcan coast, and the view from the top across the southern part of the island is excellent.

CALA D'ES TALAIER

To the west, not far from the Cala de Turqueta, is the ★ **Cala d'es Talaier**, or Guardians' Bay – perhaps the people in charge of the watchtower couldn't resist a quick dip in this bay in former times. The way eastwards is one of the nicest sections of the Camí de Cavalls, with aromatic pines, mastic trees and wild fig trees – with the sea in the background all the way.

First the path leads to ★ **Cala Macarelleta**, home to nudists and young backpackers with sleeping-bags during the summer; then on to the larger ★ **Cala Macarella**, which takes about an hour to reach. Flanked by high rocks, these bays used to be almost deserted but today are popular with those eager to flee the bustle of Cala Santa Galdana, from where they can be reached on foot through pine woodsin around 30–40 minutes *(see page 85)*. The sand is fine, the water clear and a small bar provides refreshments at Cala Macarella in high season.

Beach football, Cala Macarella

SON CATLAR

The highlight of this route is the prehistoric village of ★★★ **Son Catlar** (open daily 10am–9pm or sunset; entrance charge in summer), one of the finest on the Balearic Islands. You should take the right fork back at the Son Vivó farmhouse and go about 5km (3 miles) down a narrow, potholed road. The settlement is encircled by an 870-m (2,850-ft) wall, several metres thick, with the remains of square defensive towers and galleries and a gateway, and it was probably used most in the 3rd and 2nd centuries BC. Its origins date back to the Bronze Age, and the village was inhabited until the fall of the Roman Empire.

Within the well-preserved enclosing walls, five *talayots* and the *taula* can be made out. The coping stone on the central sanctuary caved in at some point and cracked. One of the special features of this site is the *hypogaeum*, a small underground chamber that was used for funerary purposes. The whole site is surrounded by oak, gorse and macchia, and sheep graze peacefully nearby; the view of the sea is excellent. Since the mid-1990s Son Catlar has been a UNESCO site, and there are explanatory signboards in four languages all over the place. There is also a small museum and café. As befits one of Menorca's most important monuments, it has a large car park, an information kiosk and public toilets.

SON SAURA

Continue down the same road and you will reach the idyllic bay of ★★ **Son Saura**, passing, en route,

Star Attraction
• Son Catlar

Below: going for a dip
Bottom: Son Catlar

Map on page 93

Cave paintings
An unusual place near Son Saura is a prehistoric cave that has been adorned by its denizen, an artist named Nicolau Cabrisas – a sculptor and the *enfant terrible* of the holiday village. The cave contains imaginative ornaments, sculptures and masks (May–Sept, mornings).

the almost-invisible remains of the megalithic village of **Egipte**. Son Saura has a very long, sandy beach, and its shallow waters are perfect for families with young children, with the adjacent pine forest providing welcome shade. From the eastern edge of the bay, the Cap des Talaier can be reached in 15 minutes. To reach the Cap d'Artrutx you either need to walk westwards along the beach or drive back to Ciutadella.

CALA SANTANDRIA AND OTHER BAYS

Several of the beaches on the southwest coast are strikingly beautiful, and attracted the attention of developers long ago. This explains the uninspired architecture in many places: holiday villages line up together side by side, with a few large hotels in between, and numerous bars and restaurants all competing for custom. As a result, the bays and beaches tend to get packed.

A first impression is provided by the beach at ★ **Cala Santandría**; if you can't find a space here the best thing to do is walk either north or south and try your luck at the next beach instead. The entrance to Cala Santandría is guarded by the 18th-century, British-built **Torre des Castell**.

From here it's only a stone's throw to the holiday settlement of **Cala Blanca**. Sunshades stand on the narrow beach in long lines, and high pine trees provide the apartments with shade. At the end of the bay are the remains of a prehistoric house, its ground-plan similar to that of a *naveta*. Ceramic finds have dated the place to between 2000 and 1000BC. There's a good view of the entire Menorcan west coast from the promontory of S'Aigo Dolca, located further to the south.

CAP D'ARTRUTX

As the road continues southwards it is lined by walled-in fields, and two *talayots* can be seen to the left and right. Tall heaps of stones everywhere make it clear how hard it is to farm on Menorca – it's impossible to till even a metre of land without having to remove a large number of rocks and

Santandría resort

stones first. Roughly 3km (1½ miles) beyond Cala Blanca, a footpath leads off to the left and down to the bay of Son Saura.

If visibility is reasonably good, there is an incomparable view of the peaks on Mallorca from **Cap d'Artrutx**. The distance between the two Balearic Islands is 20 nautical miles, equivalent to 37km (23 miles). The black-and-white-striped lighthouse on the island's southwestern-most point was built in 1868, but is unfortunately closed to visitors.

Star Attraction
• **Son Saura**

Below: market trader
Bottom: Cap d'Artrutx

CALA EN BOSC

The next holiday village, **Cala en Bosc**, is especially popular with package tourists because of its 300-m (985-ft) beach and excellent recreational infrastructure. Whatever you want – surfboards, sailboats, motorboats, discos, karaoke bars, hostess bars – it's all here. A new marina, a palm-lined promenade and large hotels and ethnic restaurants such as Bahia or Chinatown round off the general picture. If this place is too busy for you, take the *minitren* (a tourist train on tyres rather than rails) to the housing development at **Son Xoriguer** and discover the small beaches there, broken up by rocks. The architecture isn't that much different from the Cala en Bosc, however. Or you can set off back to Ciutadella.

Map on page 93

8: The Rugged Northwest Coast

Cala Morell – Platjes d'Algaiarens – Punta Nati – Cala en Blanes – Los Delfines – Pont d'en Gil – Ciutadella (50km/31 miles)

The difference couldn't be more striking: to the north of Ciutadella there are remote, barren and almost depressing regions while close by to the west the whitewashed holiday villages are located side by side – although the areas where mass tourism has made the most inroads tend to look rather depressing, too.

Ciutadella, the former metropolis, serves as the starting-point and end of this route. The side roads leading to the sea sometimes pass less attractive parts of Menorca, but the steep, rocky coast, up to 40m (130ft) high in places, is always an experience in itself, whether it's the Cala Morell with its weird rock formations, the Punta Nati, where a lighthouse has warned mariners of underwater dangers since 1913, or the Pont d'en Gil, a natural bridge eroded by centuries of seawater.

One special highlight of western Menorca are the *barraques*, cattle shelters that look very similar to many of the island's prehistoric structures.

Broad and seemingly endless beaches like the Platjes d'Algaiarens to the north are the exception here. The beaches west of the town are hardly worthy of the name, and holidaymakers here tend to favour their swimming pools.

Below: shade against the sun
Bottom: Cala Morell bay

LEAVING CIUTADELLA

From the centre of Ciutadella *(see page 35)*, take the Contramurada – the ring road that follows the course of the former town wall – and the road to Avinguda de La Constitució is signposted. A bumpy asphalt road leads through the industrial area of Ciutadella and then past gardens and fields edged with the drystone walls that are so typical of the island. Here in the stony northwest of the island the walls are frequently just a few metres apart. With a little luck you may see a few *pedrers* at work – the people who build and repair the walls with so much skill.

CALA MORELL

Beyond the Torre d'en Quart farm, with the medieval watchtower that once served as a defence against pirate attack, the vegetation is replaced almost entirely by a stony desert, until ★ **Cala Morell** and its tiny beach appear. The bay is surrounded by some very strange rock formations. They are part limestone and part conglomerate, and red blocks of sandstone can also be seen among them. This natural, weatherbeaten stone garden dates back to the era when mighty mountains of mud rolled here from inland and then solidified. Wind and water then did the rest. Colour contrast is provided by the sparkling white

Torre d'en Quart

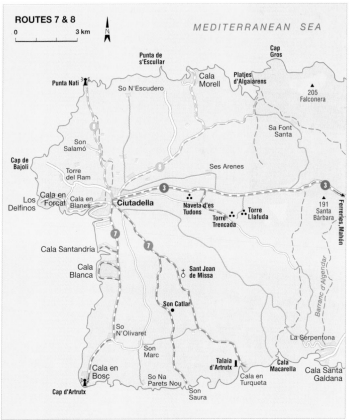

ROUTES 7 & 8

0   3 km

N

MEDITERRANEAN SEA

Cap Gros

Punta de s'Escullar

Cala Morell

Platjes d'Algaiarens

Punta Nati

So N'Escudero

▲ 205 Falconera

Sa Font Santa

Son Salamó

Cap de Bajoli

Torre del Ram

Ses Arenes

Los Delfinos

Cala en Forcat

Cala en Blanes

Ciutadella

Naveta d'es Tudons

Torre Llafuda

191 Santa Bàrbara

Ferreries, Mahón

Torre Trencada

Cala Santandria

Cala Blanca

Sant Joan de Missa

So N'Olivaret

Son Catlar

Son Marc

La Serpentona

Cala en Bosc

So Na Parets Nou

Talaia d'Artrutx

Cala en Turqueta

Cala Macarella

Cala Santa Galdana

Cap d'Artrutx

Son Saura

Barranc d'Algendar

Map on page 93

houses and lush gardens that line the broad avenues of the upmarket development of Cala Morell, set high above the bay. In the summer, boat trips are available from here along the steep coastline to the west, where you can go for lengthy clifftop walks.

A short distance up the steep road from the bay is a cave settlement established by the original inhabitants of Menorca and dating back to around 1000BC – the **Cuevas de Cala Morell** (open site; free). The settlement consists of a total of 17 caverns, believed to have been used both as residences and as tombs, or ossuaries, some of which are sub-divided into several smaller chambers. These Bronze and Iron Age caves are surprisingly refined, decorated with classical carvings and with windows cut into the rock; oval niches in the stone probably served as places to bury bones, and others to collect rainwater. The natural stone vaults of the caves look almost man-made as they spring from the floor on stout stone columns.

Below: Cala Morell caves
Bottom: Punta Nati

PLATJES D'ALGAIARENS

To the east of Cala Morell is the region of **La Vall**, the largest intact area of woodland on the island, renowned for its scenic beauty. The road leads right through the middle as far as the fine, sandy ★ **Platjes d'Algaiarens**, where twin beaches are

set in a horseshoe bay. The forests, bays and pine-lined beaches here are all privately owned, and there is a guardian on duty to ensure that traffic is limited. Up to 200 vehicles a day are allowed to pass through and use the car park near the beach – anyone in excess of that number is turned away. A toll is payable (currently €5), but it's well worth it if you want to spend a few hours, or a whole day, in this beautiful spot.

Pedestrians and cyclists are allowed through without any restrictions, however. From the car park before the toll gate, a short walk through the woods leads to the dunes from where you can clamber down onto the first beach. If this is too full, try the second or third beaches. There are no service amenities provided, nor is there any alternative way of getting back to Ciutadella – you must go back the way you came.

> **Barraques**
> One real attraction on the road to Punta Nati are the numerous *barraques* – cattle shelters resembling oversized snail-shells, built in a style reminiscent of the prehistoric *navetes* and *talayots*. Most date from the early 19th century, but some are more recent. Some *barraques* are even used as emergency accommodation by field labourers.

PUNTA NATI

If you follow the Contramurada ring road in Ciutadella as far as the caper tree-covered Bastió de Sa Font and then turn off to the right, the road to Punta Nati cannot be missed.

This trip will introduce you to some of the less pleasant aspects of Menorca. A bumpy, potholed asphalt road leads past a scrap-heap and the largest refuse dump in the west of the island, and things can get pretty nasty if the wind happens to be blowing in the wrong direction. But if you can ignore the smell, and enjoy looking at landscapes that are practically devoid of vegetation, then this region is for you. The traditional Menorcan walls are everywhere, yet again, and sheep can be seen searching the barren ground for something to graze on.

From the northern cape of ★ **Punta Nati** the lighthouse of the same name has been sending its light across the waves ever since 1913. Be warned, if the gate happens to be closed, there's nowhere to turn round. But the 40-m (130-ft) high steep cliffs provide some excellent views across land and water, as well as the waves crashing against the reefs offshore.

Punta Nati lighthouse

Below: cycling in the heat
Bottom: a greeting from
Los Delfines

BAY OF THE DEAD

If you continue eastwards, past the cattle shelters which concealed artillery positions during the Spanish Civil War, the road leads past the Cala Es Pous and the **Cala Es Morts** – the Bay of the Dead' – which was where the French steamer *Général Chanzy* was wrecked on the rocks in 1910. Only one man survived the wreck in which 151 unfortunate passengers and crew members perished. The rusty old hulk of the vessel still commemorates the tragedy today.

TOURIST ENCLAVES

On the way back to Ciutadella there's another good site for those who like all things prehistoric: opposite the scrap-yard a track leads past a cattle-shed resembling a stepped pyramid. From there a narrow path leads to a field, to the remains of a megalithic village and above all to the *talayot* of **Torre Vella**, which has an entrance.

The way to the tourist enclaves of **Cala en Blanes**, **Cala en Forcat** and **Los Delfines** is signposted from Ciutadella's Bastió de Sa Font onwards. Outside town, several cycle paths – relatively rare on Menorca – can be seen at the side of the winding road. The rocky coast is covered with holiday homes and holiday villages, largely block-booked by tour companies, where swimming pools, tennis courts, restaurants, discos and karaoke bars all blend into one vast tourism and entertainment complex. From the steep coast here there are several fine views, however: Mallorca can be seen in good weather, as can the lighthouse at Cap d'Artrutx, the southwestern-most point of the island.

BAY AND BEACHES

The bays with their miniature beaches lie at the centres of the various holiday enclaves, with the most generously-proportioned probably being the **Cala en Blanes**, which also has a small palm grove. The town of **Cala en Forcat** is grouped around the bay of the same name, with numerous natural and concrete sun terraces. Small fountains spurt out of the rock now and then – they're not volcanic, but the result of pressure changes in a subterranean system of caverns.

PONT D'EN GIL

If you walk from the Hipódromo racecourse *(see below)* on the outskirts of **Los Delfines** in a north-westerly direction along the coast for about 10 minutes, you will reach the ★**Pont d'en Gil** promontory with its large rocky gateway, which was carved out by the sea. It immediately makes you want to stop for a picnic nearby or slip through the archway on a small boat.

If you still don't feel too weary from all the walking, you could carry on to the **Cap de Bajolí** further north. A defensive tower dating from the 17th century, built here as part of an early warn-ing system against pirate incursions, will guide you on your way.

On the way back to Ciutadella, take a look at the posters outside the Hipódromo Torre del Ram. Horse races and harness races, where jockeys sit in small carts, from which they control their horses, are usually held here on Sunday evening (tel: 971 388 038), and are always well patron-ised. Bets are laid too, of course, and sometimes taken quite seriously. It's great fun to watch.

Aqua Park
If you've got young children, you can take them to the Aqua Park in Cala Forcat, where they are sure to enjoy the flumes and slides. The restaurant serves excellent pizzas and there's also a bouncy cas-tle play area. The entrance fee is for the whole day but you can come and go as you please. Open 10am–6pm, the park can be found on the main road going into Cala Forcat from Ciutadella; there is also a bus which drops you right outside the entrance.

Pont d'en Gil

Architectural heritage

If the official count is correct, there are more than 1,600 prehistoric monuments on Menorca. They include natural caverns that were inhabited over 5,000 years ago, caves cut out of limestone with great difficulty, watchtowers, funerary buildings and entire villages. There are 2½ archaeological sites per square kilometre, so Menorca can rightly be termed an open-air museum – Mallorca, Ibiza and Formentera all fall far behind. And since archaeology is a relatively young science, it can be assumed that a great deal remains to be discovered on the island. By the end of the 1940s around 500 sites were known about, but that figure had risen to 1,000 a decade later.

MEGALITHIC STRUCTURES

Menorca developed its main reputation as an archaeological treasure-trove from the megalithic structures known as *talayots, taules* and *navetas*, which were built quite independently from any cave settlements between 2000 and 800BC. During this period a civilisation developed in the Western Mediterranean that has become known on the Balearic Islands as the *Talayotic* culture.

TALAYOTS

This period was named after the *talayots* – stone towers, usually round, and up to 10m (32ft) high. The name possibly comes from *atalaya*, the Arabic word for a watchtower. Comparable to the *torri* of Corsica or the *nuraghi* of Sardinia, they were probably used not only as watchtowers but also as refuges in time of danger; they could also have provided accommodation for village elders, and subsequently served as burial sites for them.

Around 200 *talayots* have survived on Menorca. There are interesting ones in the settlements of Talati de Dalt, Torre d'en Galmes Son Catlar and Trepucó. The highest tower is the one at Torrellonet, which has been equipped with flight guidance systems for the nearby airport.

> **Cave dwellings**
> The evidence from the megalithic period raises more questions than it answers. It seems certain, however, that the first settlers sailed from the coast of Southern France and arrived on the northernmost of the Balearic Islands in around 5000BC. Natural caves in bays such as Cales Coves, Cala Morell and Cala Canutells, or the gigantic Cova d'es Coloms in the interior, all provided these early visitors with welcome accommodation. The more people they had to house, the more antechambers, niches and additional rooms were created. Many of the caves were built completely by human beings, and were used as living accommodation, burial grounds, or a mixture of the two.

*Opposite: Taula de Trepucó
Below: Talayot de Torrellonet*

The most impressive interior, complete with stone pillars and beams, can be seen at the site of Sant Agustí Vell *(see page 82)*.

TAULES

Taules (the Menorcan word for tables) are T-shaped stone structures composed of two massive stone slabs, one above the other. Over 30 of them still exist on Menorca, and lie at the centre of any megalithic settlement. Their original purpose is not known, but the *taules*, which are up to 5m (16ft) high, are always located at the very centre of horseshoe-shaped patterns of monolithic stones in temple areas, where traces of fires and benches for animal sacrifices have also been discovered. The most impressive *taules* can be seen at Torralba d'en Salort, Talatí de Dalt, Torre Trencada, Trepucó, Son Catlar and Torre Llisà Vell.

Below: Talatí de Dalt
Bottom: Naveta d'es Tudons

NAVETES

The third kind of prehistoric structure on Menorca is the *naveta,* an ossuary reminiscent of a boat lying keel-upwards, hence the name. These structures contain an antechamber, a large interment chamber on ground level and frequently a burial chamber above it. The only way to enter a *naveta* is on one's hands and knees. The amount of bones found inside them makes it likely that they were used as tribal tombs, and many contained valuable funerary offerings such as rings, amulets, necklaces and small figurines. The Navetes de Rafal Rubí and the Naveta d'es Tudons are the most remarkable monuments of their type, and the latter is also believed to be the oldest structure in the whole of Spain.

LATER DEVELOPMENTS

There are few remnants of classical antiquity on Menorca, but both the Greeks and the Phoenicians left behind evidence of trading activity in the form of jewellery, utensils and coins. The Phoenicians and the Romans had great respect for the

Balearides (the name given to the islanders because of their throwing ability – *ballein* is the Greek word for throw). The sling was a vital weapon the islanders employed against foreign foes, and the slingsmen of Menorca were recruited as mercenaries, constituting an important division in Hannibal's armies as well as in the Roman force that conquered Carthage in 143BC.

ROMANS, CHRISTIANS AND MOORS

Under Quintus Caecilius Metellus, the Romans finally conquered the islands in 123BC. They fortified the local strongholds, constructed villas, baths and temples, and of course built their roads, such as the one that can still be seen on Puig de Santa Agueda *(see page 59)*. After the collapse of the Roman Empire, the Balearics were subjected to continuous plundering, and it was only after 1025 that a new cultural heyday emerged under the Moors. However, not many Arab buildings survived the Christian conquest at the beginning of the 13th century; most of them were either destroyed or incorporated into new structures. Ciutadella's main mosque, for example, became the Gothic cathedral. The Gothic pointed arch replaced the horseshoe arch of the Moors, but the Spanish did adopt the Moorish idea of arcaded courtyards and fountains, where water allowed.

> **Mystery of the *taules***
> How the incredibly heavy stones of the *taules* were placed on top of each other and connected without any technological assistance remains a mystery to this day, as does their significance. Did they represent deities, or were they used to mark cult sites?

Eglesia del Roser in Ciutadella

In the Middle Ages, most building activity was of a religious nature, but later on magnificent secular buildings were constructed by merchants, landowners and wealthy artisans. Townhouses and *palazzi* were built in Ciutadella. With their richly decorated façades and beautiful courtyards, these buildings represented a fusion of the many different styles that came together in the Balearics, and some of them can still be admired today.

Menorca's Farmhouses

Crossing Menorca, you can't fail to notice all the white-washed farmhouses. Some might dominate a hilltop while others occupy a more modest position, stooped low against the ground as if cowering against the elements – braced for an onslaught of the north wind, the *Tramuntana*. But whatever their location, these farmhouses all share a distinctive Menorcan style of architecture.

The central yards of these *llocs* are invariably surrounded by several buildings, which is why the locals refer to them in the plural, as *ses cases* – the houses. The northern side is usually occupied by outbuildings such as stables and dairies, which help protect the rest of the farm from the elements. Living quarters always face south, as does the patio area, which is usually furnished with a well, an oven for baking, a water trough and a round threshing floor made of brick. The entire complex is surrounded by a dry-stone wall.

Also typical is the protruding triple-arched porch area *(sa porxada)*; in the summer this is the focus of family life and in winter the venue for traditional livestock slaughtering and festivities *(matanzas)*. The roof of this porch doubles as a terrace. The shallow gable roof is in the typical Spanish style with terracotta tiles; terracotta pipes carry the water to underground storage cisterns.

The *llocs* are built of large limestone slabs *(marés)* obtained from the island's quarries. As the limestone is porous and lacks water resistance, the walls are treated with a coat of whitewash once a year, adding flashes of brightness to Menorca's already broad spectrum of colours.

Below: Ciutadella townhouses

Festivals

Steeped in centuries of tradition, Menorca's festivals are spectacular events, including fireworks, horse dancing and processions.

January 17: Fests d'es Tres Tocs, or festival of the three blows, held in Ciutadella to commemorate the *Reconquista* of Menorca in 1287.

March/April: Semana Santa, or Easter Week, at its most impressive in Maó and Ciutadella: religious celebrations and processions.

June 23–24: Festes de Sant Joan, the festival of St John, held in Ciutadella. Two days of equestrian fun, including the *jaleo* (horses' dance) on the Plaça d'es Born, which is crowned by a magnificent fireworks display. This is Menorca's most lively festival *(see also page 37)*.

July 15–16: boat processions in Maó, Ciutadella and Fornells. In the island's harbours the **Verge del Carmen**, the patron saint of mariners and fishermen, is celebrated in colourful processions. On the third weekend in July is the **Festa de Sant Martí,** or festival of St Martin, with horseback processions and tournaments plus the traditional *jaleo*. On the fourth weekend is the **Festa de Sant Antoni** in Antonells in honour of the patron saint. The processions are crowned by a magnificent *jaleo* at the harbour.

August: A whole series of local **patron saint celebrations**, featuring processions and, especially, markets. The first weekend has celebrations in Es Migjorn Gran, the second in Alaior, the third in Sant Climent and the fourth in Sant Lluís, while Ferreries celebrates its saint on 24–25 August.

September 7–9: Festes de la Verge de Gràcia, the festival of the Holy Virgin of Monte Toro, held in Maó; processions and a horseback parade with around 100 horses, all crowned by the biggest fireworks display on the island.

Below: jaleo in Ciutadella
Bottom: Festes de Gràcia figure
Overleaf: local restaurant sign

FOOD AND DRINK

Menorca has a vast number of culinary delights. The overladen market stalls in the Claustre del Carme in Maó or at the Mercat in Ciutadella prompt you to visit the nearest gourmet restaurant, especially in Es Mercadal or Es Migjorn Gran. Many meals begin with fresh bread and a small bowl of *ali-oli*, mayonnaise in its original form *(see overleaf)*. Avoid establishments advertising 'international cooking', as this often means there will be pizza, chips and hamburgers on the menu.

SEAFOOD ASSORTMENT

Top of the popularity list are the seafood dishes, especially *caldereta de langosta* (or *llagosta* in *menorquí*), which is especially good in the restaurants of Fornells. A thick soup is prepared over high heat using tomatoes, onions, garlic, parsley, leeks, a little cognac, and thinly sliced lobster, then poured onto slices of bread and served. Each cook refines the dish differently according to a personal recipe. The only disadvantage of this superb dish is the price – around €50 (price categories in the restaurant listings do not include choosing this dish).

The *caldereta* family also includes two cheaper dishes, however: *caldereta de mariscos*, a shellfish soup, and *caldereta de pescado*, which contains several different kinds of fish. *Lubina* (sea bass), *dorado* (gilthead bream) and *besugo* (sea bream) are also on many menus, grilled *(a la plancha)* or in the oven *(al horno)*. They are sometimes prepared in an outer casing of sea salt before being baked A typically Menorcan variant is to bake the fish in the oven with potatoes and halved tomatoes.

Anyone who is eager to try a number of different kinds of fish should sample a *parillada de pescado*, which is varied and delicious. The island's cooks are just as good at shellfish and crustaceans: squid, mussels and sea-snails are all expertly prepared.

Paella, the most popular tourist dish, can contain both fish *(paella marinera)* and meat. However, the classic ones usually feature saffron rice, chicken, pork, mussels, shrimps, cuttlefish, beans and peas.

FURTHER SPECIALITIES

Like their colleagues on the mainland, Menorcan cooks use a lot of onions,

Mahón Cheese

If the souvenir shops had anything to do with it, every visitor to Menorca would take home at least one *Queso de Mahón*. Regardless of the aroma and oppressive summer heat, no souvenir shop would be complete without a row of these colourfully packed cheeses.

Some of Menorca's cheese is still made by small family businesses, but most is now produced on a large scale. Since 1985, it has all carried the official label *Queso de Mahón*, although Alaior is actually the centre of production. Despite mechanisation, the cheese is still made in the traditional manner, except that cows' milk rather than sheep milk is used. First, the whey is separated from the set milk using muslin. The cheese is then soaked for a day in salt water and left on a rack for a month, where it is turned. A mix of butter, olive oil and paprika is then applied to the surface, and two months later the cheese is ready. According to maturity, the taste varies from tangy to spicy and the colour from deep yellow to ivory. After eight months it has a similar texture to parmesan.

Queso de Mahón is best bought either straight from the farm or from a factory outlet in Alaior. You won't get the colourful packaging but you may get a glimpse of the cellars, and the price is lower than in souvenir shops.

garlic and olive oil, but these are enhanced by local ingredients such as *Queso de Mahón (see previous page).* Ingredients common to many meat dishes include capers, figs, cabbage, beans and artichokes. The meat ranges from pork and beef to rabbit, quail and partridge.

Whether it's *conejo con higos* (rabbit with dried figs) or *cordero con cebollas y alcaparras* (lamb with onions and capers), these oven-baked dishes are among the true highlights of Menorcan cuisine – especially if you happen to order them from the Ca n'Aguedet restaurant in Es Mercadal or El Gallo near Ferreries.

Special island delicacies include stuffed aubergines, peppers, courgettes and artichokes as well as the numerous simple soups enjoyed by the rural population. One such soup, *oli-aigua,*consisting of tomatoes, onions, cabbage and toasted bread comes in all kinds of variations. *Sopas mallorquinas* – a Mallorcan dish always referred to in this plural form – is a combination of vegetables, olives, garlic and sometimes pork, more like a stew than a soup. *Trempó* is usually described as a salad but it can be more like a rather solid *gazpacho. Tumbet* is a dish of peppers, aubergines, tomatoes and potatoes, coated in beaten egg and baked. .

Tapas, the famous Spanish appetisers, can be found in all variations on Menorca. Portions of fried squid , *albóndigas* (meat balls), spicy *chorizo,* and *butifarrone,* white or black sausages, are among the most famous. Tapas are often accompanied by *pa amb tomàquet,* bread rubbed with oil, garlic and tomato. Good snacks, which are also eaten as desserts, include *amargos* (almond-flavoured biscuits) and *ensaimadas* (yeast cakes fried in lard and topped with icing sugar), which are popular for breakfast.

THE SECRET OF MAYONNAISE

Mayonnaise – *mahonesa* – was invented on Menorca. In 1756 the French had just driven the British (temporarily) from the island, and their leader, the Duke of Richelieu, wanted to celebrate the occasion. A local cook created a delicious, thick sauce with eggs, olive oil, lemon and garlic, known as *alioli.* The French took the recipe to Paris, but left out the garlic.

In another version of the story, the cook was a mistress of Richelieu's. In memory of his amorous escapade, he is reputed to have named this culinary speciality after the place where he met the *mahonesa* he had loved.

DRINKS

If you need something to settle your stomach after all this indulgence, try the *hierbas* – herbal liqueur that tastes of camomile – or *calent,* an aniseed, cinnamon and saffron liqueur that is drunk warm. *Palo* – a bitter-tasting brew made of gentian extract and various herbs – is regarded as a stimulant. For something really refreshing, there is *Pomada,* the local *Xoriguer* gin, served in a 1:3 mixture with lemonade.

Restaurant selection

Restaurants have been sub-divided into three approximate price categories (for a 3-course meal for one with house wine): **€€€** = €45–75, **€€** = €30–45, **€** = under €30.

Alaior

The Cobblers, Carrer d'en Macarí 6, tel: 971 371 400. An English-run restaurant in a converted cobbler's shop, with good meat dishes and excellent salads. Pretty courtyard. **€€**

Biniancolla

Biniancolla, tel: 908 099 061. Large restaurant with terrace above the bay, great for dining at sunset, lots of seafood, and great *paella*. €€

Binibeca Vell

El Pescadito, tel: 971 188 543. Pleasant place with vaulted ceiling, and large selection of fresh fish. €€

Cala Blanca

Es Caliu, Carretera Ciutadella–Cala en Bosc, tel: 971 380 165. A large, busy restaurant specialising in good barbecued meat. €€

Cala en Bosc

Café Balear, El Lago, tel: 608 744 816. Sister to the Balear in Ciutadella (*see below*), deservedly popular for grilled meats and fish. €€

Cala Santa Galdana

Es Barranc, Passeig Marítim s/n, tel: 971 154 643. Right at the entrance to the Barranc d'Algendar, and the food is good despite the uninspired décor. Try the *Cap Roig con ajos* (scorpion fish with garlic). €€
El Mirador, tel: 908 799 847. Uninspiring mass fare, and off-hand service, but the location on a promontory in the bay is utterly superb. €

Ciutadella

Café Balear, Marina s/n, tel: 971 380 005. Does an excellent *caldereta de llagost*a and good fishy starters. €€
Casa Manolo, Marina 117, tel: 971 380 003. Long-established and popular seafood place at the far end of the harbour, with air-conditioning, terrace and magnificent views. €€–€€€
D'es Port, Carrer Marina 23, tel: 971 480 022. Set into the cliff and with tables on the quayside, this smart blue-and-white restaurant serves excellent fish, including *suquet* (fish stew) and *esqueixada*, a salad of tomatoes, onions and salt cod. €€€

El Bribón, Marina 115, tel: 971 38 50 50. One of the best-known restaurants in the harbour. Well-prepared fish dishes. €
La Guitarra, Carrer dels Dolors 1,tel: 971 381 355. A place worth leaving the harbour for. Close to the Plaça de la Catedral this well-run cellar restaurant serves authentic *cuina menorquina,* including *conejo con cebolla*s (rabbit with onions). €€

Es Mercadal

Ca n'Aguedet, Carrer Lepanto 23–30, tel: 971 375 391. Some of the best *cuina menorquina* on the island at surprisingly reasonable prices. Excellent rabbit *(conejo)*, lamb *(cordero)* and suckling pig *(lechona)*. The owners also produce the only wine on the island. Booking recommended. €€
Ca n'Olga, Pont Na Macarrana, tel: 971 375 459. Hidden away behind an arch near the Torrente, with large garden terrace and stylish furnishings; very good Menorcan food, especially the seafood, quail *(cordoniz)* and rabbit *(conejo)*. Booking advisable. €€
Molis d'es Reco, Carrer Vicario Fuxà 53, tel: 971 375 392. An old mill with a large terrace, on the C721. It specialises in catering to large coach parties so can get very busy. €€

> **Water and wine**
> The water in Menorca is perfectly safe to drink but it has a rather distinctive taste. Most people drink bottled water – *agua mineral*. If you want it sparkling, ask for *agua con gas*, while still water is *agua sin gas*. *Fresca* means chilled, *natural* means straight off the shelf. Wine is usually drunk with meals, but as there is only one local producer – the Vadell family who own the Ca n'Aguedet *(see above)*, it nearly all comes from mainland Spain. Beer, both bottled and draught, is more popular with younger people.

Es Migjorn Gran

Migjorn, Carrer Major, tel: 971 370 112. House with small courtyard terrace and Menorcan dishes, all refined in an interesting way. €

58, S'Engolidor, Carrer Major 3, tel: 971 370 193. Small, atmospheric place a view over the gorge. serving great Menorcan dishes, including *dorado con alcaparras* (gilthead bream with capers). Reservations essential. €€

Ferreries

El Gallo, Cta Cala Santa Galdana, tel: 971 373 039. Old farmhouse restaurant serving good grilled meat. €€

Fornells

Es Cranc, Carrer Escoles 31, tel: 971 376 442. Tucked away in the old town Es Cranc serves imaginative meat and fish dishes. Book at weekends. €€

El Pescador, Plaça s'Algaret 3, tel: 971 376 538. Ceramic plates with crustacean motifs on the walls, a pleasant terrace and a huge fish menu. €€

Es Pla, Pasaje des Plá, tel: 971 376 655. Tastefully decorated restaurant right by the water. This is where Juan Carlos orders his *caldereta* when the royal yacht anchors nearby. €€

Sa Llagosta, Carrer Gabriel Gelabert 12, tel: 971 376 566. Smart, discreet establishment. Serves calamares with green risotto, and baked fish, as well as *caldereta de llagosta* and lobster in other guises. €€€

Maó

Andaira, Carrer des Forn 61, tel: 971 366 817. The Andaira serves interesting Mediterranean dishes in a green-shuttered townhouse with a courtyard, close to Plaça de s'Esplanada. Dinner only. €€–€€€

Il Porto, Moll de Llevant 225, tel: 971 354 426. Relaxed atmosphere, good grilled vegetables. Try *pimientos de padrón* (small, green peppers). €

Gregal, Moll de Llevant 306, tel: 971 366 606. At the Cala Figuera end of the harbour this restaurant produces a range of imaginative fish dishes, and is a great local favourite. Try the *merluza* (hake), served on a bed of black rice. €€

La Minerva, Moll de Llevant 87, tel: 971 351 995. The main restaurant is set in an old flour mill, but you can also eat on the floating jetty. Elegant and expensive, but there's an excellent-value *menú del día*. €€

La Sirena, Moll de Llevant 199, tel: 971 350 740. A German-owned, vegetarian-friendly restaurant, where organic produce is used as much as possible. €€

Roma, Moll de Llevant 295, tel: 971 353 777. Most popular pizzeria in Maó; cheerful and always busy. €

Sant Tomàs

Es Bruc, Carretera San Adeoato, tel: 971 370 488. Meals and tapas on a large terrace above the beach. €

Sant Climent

Casino Sant Climent, Carrer de Sant Jaume 4, tel: 971 153 418. Simple food, served to the accompaniment of good jazz on Tuesday and Thursday, when musicians are welcome to bring their own instruments and join in. €

Sant Lluís

Pan y Vino, Carrer Torret 52, tel: 971 150 322. In the village of Torret, near Sant Lluís, this is *the* place for Menorcan cuisine and select wines. Elegant, intimate, and very popular with the local expatriate population. €€€

El Picadero, Ctra Maó–San Lluís, tel: 971 363 268. British-run restaurant with lots of barbecued meat. €€

La Venta de Paco, Carrer de Sant Lluís s/n, tel: 971 150 995. Rustic furnishings and good *cuina menorquina*, including *cabrito* (kid). €€

ACTIVE HOLIDAYS

BEACHES

Despite some wonderful hiking routes and the 9-hole golf course at Son Bou, the sea is naturally the focal point of tourist interest on Menorca.

The island has bays and beaches to suit every taste, and they really are picturesque. There are huge differences, however: on the Platja de Son Bou or the Cala Santa Galdana with their high-rise hotels, be prepared to share the beach with many others. Things are far quieter on the beaches known as *platjes verges* to the southeast of Ciutadella. Not all the beaches can be easily reached by car, and the last section often has to be done on foot. Bays like Cala en Turqueta, Cala des Talaier or Son Saura are worth walking to, in any case. Topless sunbathing is a common sight now (but do cover up when you leave the beach); nudism is still only possible in the most remote bays such as Cala Macarellata.

HIKING

Menorca is ideal for short or long hikes, and it's easy to orient yourself according to landmarks like Monte Toro or the Puig de Santa Àgueda. The best starting points for hikes are Fer-

reries, Cala Santa Galdana, Alaior, Es Mercadal and Fornells. Many of the routes are not properly marked, however, and even expensive maps leave a lot to be desired.

For information on guided walks, contact the Oficina d'Informació Turística in Maó and Ciutadella *(see page 113)*. Bird-watching trips and other nature tours are organised by the GOB, Carrer d'Isabel II 42, Maó, tel: 971 350 763. Dia Complert Esport d'Aventura, Carrer des Forn 33, Maó; tel: 609 670 996, arranges hiking and biking routes all over the island, including bird-watching excursions. Hiking in the Barranc d'Algendar can be organised in Cala Santa Galdana through the Hotel Audax, tel: 971 154 646, which has a kiosk on the Passeig Marítim. For all kinds of outdoor activities, check Menorcaactiva, tel: 971 352 464, www.menorcaactiva.com

Parts of the Camí de Cavalls *(see page 11)*, can be walked, often through remote regions of great natural beauty. If you are crossing private property, be sure to close all gates behind you.

Surfing and swiming at Cala N'Porter

CYCLING

Bikes can be hired from several shops in Ciutadella, Maó and most of the resorts. They cost around €5 a day. Mountain bikes are the best bet because quite a few roads and beach-access tracks are incredibly bumpy. You don't need to be particularly athletic, however. The old Camí d'en Kane *(see page 50)* is easy and quiet.

RIDING

On Menorca, horses are either bred for racing or used as work animals; riding is purely for visitors. Riding trips are available from around 20 stables, including the Rancho Allenwood, tel: 971 153 071, near Sant Climent and Club Hipic es Boeret, tel: 971 151 0 9, at S'Algar. Menorca en Cavall, tel: 971 154 123, at Cala Santa Galdana organises treks through nearby woodlands. The Hort de Llucaitx Park, Carretera Maó–Fornells Km 17, tel: 629 392 894, also has horses and ponies for hire and is a good bet for children.

WATERSPORTS

Menorca is ideal for windsurfers and sailors, whether beginners, keen amateurs or experts. The holiday centres and marinas in the south of the island are the best places to head for. Punta Prima (near Maó) and Cala en Bosc (near Ciutadella) are both very good for windsurfing. Fornells has a yacht club that offers surfing courses and rents out equipment, and it is perfectly located on a long bay. The club also has a sailing school and 50 berths.

The larger towns are also popular with watersports enthusiasts: Surf & Sail, tel: 971 387 090, in Ciutadella, organises all kinds of watersports activities for all abilities. Club Marítimo de Maó, tel: 971 365 022, is a good sailing school. The most ambitious of all is S'Algar Aguasports, tel: 971 15 0 601, in Cala d'Alcaufar,

where you can learn anything from windsurfing to water-skiing and parasailing. Divers should try The Diving Centre, Cala Torret, tel: 971 188 528, which offers introductions to scuba as well as daily diving trips. Diving Center Fornells, Passeig Marítim 44B, Fornells, tel: 971 376 431, is a recommended organisation, as are.SUBmorena Divers, Passeig de la Riu, Loc. 7, Cala Galdana, tel: 971 154 657; and Ulmo Diving Centre Addaia, tel: 971 359 005; www.ulmodiving.com, which runs trips for qualified divers and courses for beginners,

Nightlife

Nightlife roughly falls into two categories: the loud late-night action in the bigger resorts, where you will rub shoulders almost exclusively with other tourists; and the more indigenous spots, mostly in Maó and Ciutadella. The island's discos come and go in the popularity stakes (and are only open in summer). Things don't get moving until late: some places don't open until 11pm but once open, they keep going.

A few bars and clubs that have stood the test of time are:

Asere, Carrer Capllonc 15, Ciutadella, tel: 971 383 852. Lively salsa club, with Cuban cocktails.

Casino Sant Climent, Carrer de Sant Jaume 4, Sant Climent, tel: 971 153 418. Good jazz sessions on Tuesday and Thursday. Musicians are welcome to bring their own instruments and join in.

Cova d'en Xoroi, tel: 971 377 236, the most famous disco on the island, set in the cliffs in Cala N'Porter.

Jazzbah, Plaça Sant Joan 3, Ciutadella (tel: 971 485 329).

The only casino on the island is the **Casino Marítim**, Moll de Llevant 288, Maó (tel: 971 364 962) where you can play the tables and machines from 9pm–5am. Dress smartly and bring your passport for identification purposes.

PRACTICAL INFORMATION

Getting There

BY AIR

Menorca's airport (about 7km/4 miles from Maó) is linked by regular scheduled flights with London, Berlin, Frankfurt and other European cities but some of them, including Iberia flights, may go via Barcelona or Palma. British Airways flies direct from Gatwick to Maó and Monarch direct from Gatwick, Luton and Manchester. Flights from the US and Canada go via Barcelona or Madrid and then on to Palma for a connecting flight.

For scheduled flights from the UK, check the website of Opodo, (www.opodo.com), which finds the best flights operated by a number of major airlines. In the US, contact Iberia, tel: 1-800 772 4642, www.iberia.com/ibusa; or British Airways, tel: 1-800 247 9297, www.britishairways.com

Easyjet, www.easyjet.com, flies from UK airports to Palma from where you get a connecting flight. Check the Internet for availability. Flights from Palma to Maó take 45 minutes and cost around €95 return.

Travelling independently, choosing your own airline and hotel, usually works out more expensive than booking on a package tour because you lose the benefit of discounts that tour operators can negotiate.

BY SEA

Travelling overland to Barcelona and then on to Menorca by boat is time-consuming and expensive, but if you're driving to Spain and feel like extending your holiday with a quick trip to Menorca, it is quite feasible. Taking your own car to Menorca only starts to pay off after around five days, however, because of the relatively high ferry price and the fact that hire cars are quite cheap (roughly €25 a day, if booked in advance).

In summer there are daily direct links from Barcelona to Maó and Ciutadella via Trasmediterránea (tel: 902 454 645 in Barcelona; 971 366 050 in Menorca; www.trasmediterranea.es. – journey time about 5 hours. Off-season the service runs three times a week. There is also a daily Baleària connecting service in summer between Barcelona and Ciutadella on the new fast ferry, *Ramon Llull* and the slower *Bahía de Málaga* (tel: 902 160 180; www.balearia.net).

Passenger ferries from Mallorca run between Cala Ratjada and Ciutadella (Cape Balear Cruceros, tel: 902 100 444/971 818 517, www.cape-balear.com). The journey takes about 75 minutes. Iscomar (tel: 902 119 128; www.iscomar. com) run twice-daily car ferries (except Saturday) from Port d'Alcúdia to Ciutadella (2 hours 45 minutes).

Getting Around

BY BUS

There is no railway on the island but the bus system is comprehensively structured. Regular buses connect Maó and Ciutadella, with intermediate stops in Alaior, Es Mercadal and Ferreries, from where you can reach the southern resorts, although you may have a long wait for a connecting bus. Prices are relatively cheap, and tickets are sold on the buses. Fewer buses operate on Sunday. In Maó, most buses start from the terminal behind Plaça de s'Esplanada – where there are ambitious plans for a new terminal. It is hoped that this will be completed by the end of 2005. Contact Transportes Menorca (TMSA) in Maó, tel: 971 360 475; in Ciutadella, tel: 971 380 393. In Ciutadella, most services commence in Plaça des Pins (beside Plaça d'es Born); again, a new terminal is planned.

BY HIRE CAR, MOPED OR VESPA

Hiring a car obviously gives you more freedom and enables you to reach some attractions that would otherwise be inaccessible (such as many of the prehistoric sites). The island has few roads, however, and they get crowded in summer, especially the main C721 across the centre. Spanish fuel prices are somewhat cheaper than in Britain. A hire car costs from around €25 a day for the smallest model, booked in advance, while a moped or a Vespa will set you back around €12. Third-party insurance is included by law, but comprehensive insurance – *todo riesgo* – will be extra. Insurance may not cover you for off-road driving, even in a four-wheel-drive vehicle. You need your national driving licence, passport and a credit card.

All the major international rental companies (Avis, Hertz and Europcar) have offices at the airports, as well as in Maó, Ciutadella and the various holiday resorts, as do reputable Spanish agencies. In Alaior, Es Castell and Es Mercadal the main providers are local firms. In the summer months it is advisable to pre-book your car hire before leaving home – this can be done cheaply via the Internet. Mopeds and Vespas, on the other hand, are usually available without advance reservation.

Rules of the Road

Driving is on the right and seatbelts are obligatory both in the front and back. Speed limits are 90km/h (56mph) on main roads, 50km/h (32mph) on minor roads, and 40km/h (25mph), unless otherwise marked, in populated areas. Traffic police frequently stop drivers.

BY TAXI

The taxi drivers on Menorca have lists of fares for most routes, and they compare favourably with those in most European countries. Cabs can be found in marked ranks in most towns and resorts. Hotel receptionists are usually happy to call a taxi for you.

Facts for the Visitor

ENTRY REQUIREMENTS

British citizens and citizens of the US, Australia and New Zealand need a passport to enter Spain, while visitors from other EU countries require only a valid national identity card. For stays of more than 90 days, residence permits are required. Applications can be made at the Aliens Office in the appropriate province.

CUSTOMS

Duty-free allowances on imports from EU countries no longer exist, but do still apply to goods bought outside the EU. There are no restrictions on importing duty-paid goods bought in the EU provided they are for personal consumption. Duty-free allowances for non-EU travellers to Spain are 200 cigarettes (or 50 cigars), one litre of alcohol, 2 litres of wine, 250ml eau-de-cologne and 50g perfume.

There are no limits on the amount of money, Spanish or foreign, that you may import, although you should declare sums over the equivalent of €30,000.

TOURIST INFORMATION

The Spanish National Tourist Office will supply holiday information. Spanish National Tourist Office, 79 New Cavendish Street, London W1W 6XB, tel: 020 7486 8077, fax: 020

7486 8034; brochure line, tel: 09063 640 630 (office not open to the public except by appointment); e-mail: info.londres@tourspain.es; www.tourspain.co.uk New York: 666 Fifth Avenue, New York, NY 10103; tel: 212-265 8822, fax: 212-265 8864; e-mail: nueva york@tourspain.es; www. okspain.org Menorca: Oficina d'Informació Turística, Carrer Sa Rovellada de Dalt 24, Maó, tel: 971 363 790, fax: 971 366 056; Airport , tel: 971 157 115; Oficina d'Informació Turística, Plaça de la Catedral, Ciutadella, tel: 971 382 693.

CURRENCY AND EXCHANGE

Spain's monetary unit is the euro (abbreviated €), which is divided into 100 cents. Bank notes are in denominations of 500, 200, 100, 50, 20, 10 and 5 euros. There are coins for 1 and 2 euros and for 50, 20, 10, 5, 2 and 1 cent.

The easiest way to obtain cash is with a credit or debit card and a PIN number at one of the many ATM machines *(telebancos)* on the island. Many shops and most restaurants and hotels accept credit cards, mainly MasterCard, Eurocard and Visa, but it is wise to check in advance. Practically all Spanish banks will change foreign currency and travellers' cheques. They offer the best rates and little or no commission, but rates can vary from bank to bank so it is worth shopping around. Always take your passport when you go to change cheques or money.

TIPPING

Many restaurants now add a 10 percent tip to the bill; look for the words *servicio incluido*; if not, add 10 percent. In a bar or café it is usual to leave a few coins for the waiter. Hotel chamber-maids expect a sum appropriate to your length of stay, porters around 50 cents per item of luggage. When travelling by taxi, add 10 percent or else round up the fare.

OPENING TIMES

Shops are usually open from 9.30am to 1.30pm and 5– 8pm, Saturday until 1pm. Supermarkets often stay open all day until 10pm. Museums keep roughly the same hours as shops.

Banks open Monday to Friday 9am–1 or 2pm, but *bureaux de change* have longer opening hours, and sometimes open on Saturday morning.

Post offices open Monday to Saturday 9am–1.30pm. Main post offices in Maó and Ciutadella also open 4–6pm.

PUBLIC HOLIDAYS

1 January (New Year's Day), 6 January (Epiphany), 17 January (Sant Antoni; commemoration of the *reconquista* in 1287), 1 May (Labour Day),

---

Arts and crafts

The sheer variety of Menorcan arts and crafts can be appreciated at the fairs and markets in Ciutadella and Maó: tables covered with hand-made shoes, sandals and belts; fashion jewellery; studded handbags; plus jugs, plates and amphorae, and the prices are usually very reasonable.

The traditional Menorcan leather sandals called *abarcas* are very popular and now come in a variety of different colours. In Maó you can have them made to order in the colour of your choice in a workshop called simply S'Abarca on the Moll de Llevant.

Menorcan potters make a great variety of products. Their trademarks are the *bótils* and *ollas* – clay bottles and pots in different shapes and sizes, with unglazed exteriors. Several more colourful types have historically based patterns and ornamentation on the outside; many of the plates and pots have island landscapes on them. If you want to watch potters and painters at work, go to the Moll de Ponent in Maó's harbour and look for Hermanos Lora Buzón and S'Alambic.

25 July (Santiago/Sant Jaume, Spain's patron saint), 15 August (Assumption), 12 October (Día de la Hispanidad), 1 November (All Saints'), 8 December (Immaculate Conception), 25–26 December (Christmas). There are also several moveable feasts such as Maundy Thursday, Good Friday, Easter Monday, Whit Monday (late May) and Corpus Christi (late June).

Sant Joan

The feast of Sant Joan, described on page 37, isn't an official public holiday, but don't expect anything to be functioning normally in Ciutadella, where ordinary life in the town grinds to a halt.

Post

Stamps *(sellos)* are available from the post offices *(correos)* in Maó, Ciutadella, Alaior and Es Castell, from tobacconists *(estancos/tabacs)* all over the island, and from many places that sell postcards.

Telephoning

The code for Spain is 00 34. To dial the UK from Spain, prefix your number with 00 44 and omit the first zero from the area code.

The easiest way to make a phone call is at a Telefónica office where you make your call and pay afterwards. It is possible to make international calls from public telephones. Phonecards *(tarjetas telefónicas)* can be purchased at kiosks, post offices and tobacconists. Reduced tariffs for international calls apply from 10pm to 8am and all day Sunday.

If you are using a US credit phone card, dial the company's access number below, then 01, and then the country code. Sprint tel: 900 99 0013; AT&T tel: 900 99 0011; MCI/Worldphone tel: 900 99 0014.

Time

Spain is one hour ahead of Greenwich Mean Time (GMT +1). Summer time (GMT + 2) lasts from late March until the last Sunday in September.

Newspapers

Newsagents in Maó, Ciutadella and main resorts keep a good supply of English newspapers and the English-language *Majorca Daily Bulletin* has a Menorca section. Menorcans read the Spanish dailies *El País* and *El Mundo* to complement the island papers, the *Diario Insular, Diario de Mallorca* or *Diario 16 Baleares.*

Electricity

The usual voltage in hotels and holiday apartments is 220AC. Plugs are two-pin and a continental adaptor is essential for visitors from Britain. US visitors will need a transformer unless they have dual-voltage appliances.

Medical Assistance

All major tourist centres have *centros medicos*, where minor problems can be dealt with promptly; they usually require immediate payment. Hotel receptionists will help organise medical care in case of illness, too.

Main hospitals are: Verge del Toro, Carrer de Barcelona 2, Maó, tel: 971 157 771; Clínica Menorca, Canonge Moll, Ciutadella, tel: 971 480 505.

There are doctors surgeries (*Centros de Salud*) in the main towns, as well as dentists *(dentistas)* and pharmacists *(farmácias)*. Pharmacists are highly trained and can dispense some drugs that would be available only on prescription in England.

Emergencies

General emergencies 112; Ambulance 061; Municipal Police: 092; National Police 091; Guardia Civil: 062; Fire Brigade: 080.

ACCOMMODATION

To maintain a green, eco-friendly image and take tourism more upmarket, Menorca has increased its standards: higher-quality facilities have replaced some of those geared to mass tourism, and building restrictions are in force everywhere. You must book well in advance if you want to find accommodation during the peak season. The season runs from May to September and peaks in July and August. Many hotels close in the winter.

ENDLESS VARIETY

Accommodation on offer ranges from luxury hotels to private holiday homes, modern club villages and simple boarding houses. Categories and stars are not a very reliable guide to the quality – the ugly concrete high-rise hotels at Son Bou, for instance, all products of the construction boom in the 1970s, are high-category establishments, because of the facilities they offer, while one-star hotels like the Almirante in Es Castell or the boarding house S'Engolidor in Es Migjorn Gran, with its nostalgic charm and family-run atmosphere, can be far more pleasant places to stay and are far less expensive.

VILLAS AND HOLIDAY HOMES

The best type of holiday accommodation for families on Menorca is that provided by the innumerable private villas and holiday homes, most of them British-owned and rented out via travel agencies. You can expect two to three bedrooms, a kitchen, a comfortable living room, a terrace and usually a swimming pool too. The houses are almost all beside the sea, but whatever the brochures might promise, don't expect remote locations. They are mainly in residential areas, with a tiny piece of lawn and a few palm trees providing some privacy, and are sufficient for most self-catering visitors.

HOTELS AND APARTMENTS

The above comments about holiday homes also apply to the numerous apartments on the island, which are usually attached to hotels – so called Aparthotels – offering all the usual hotel amenities but giving you the privacy of your own rooms. The club villages close to the coasts like S'Algar or Son Parc provide similar amenities, combining sports, excursions and

Chatting in Ciutadella

accommodation. Most hotels are along the south coast, and are marketed by package tour operators. Those listed below cater, at least partially, to independent visitors.

Ciutadella and Maó provide a variety of accommodation, from *hostals* to first-class hotels; in the centre of the island there's a lot less choice. In towns like Es Migjorn Gran, Es Mercada or Ferreries, for instance, there are only one or two *hostales* available. They tend to be far away from the tourist centres, with clean, simple rooms, moderate prices and restaurants attached.

> **Rural alternative**
> An alternative is offered by Agroturismo − accommodation in country houses. Information from tourist offices in Maó and Ciutadella (*see page 113*), or from Agroturisme Balear, Av. Gabriel Alomar i Villalonga 8a, Palma, tel: 971 721 508, fax: 971 727 317.

CAMPING

S'Atalaia campsite, tel: 971 373 095, on the road from Ferreries to Cala Santa Galdana, is open all year. **Son Bou**, tel: 971 372 605, on the Platja de Son Bou, is open Apr–Oct.

Hotel selection

The following hotels have been subdivided into three approximate price categories (for a double room in high season): €€€ = 120–150, €€ = 70–150, € = under 70.

Cala Blanca

Cala Blanca, Urbanización Cala Blanca, tel: 971 380 450, fax: 971 382 000. Large hotel on the edge of the development, surrounded by palms and pines, with a swimming pool. €€
Mediterrani, Urbanización Cala Blanca, tel: 971 384 203, fax: 971 386 162. High-rise, modern and comfortable; close to the beach. €€

Cala en Bosc

Cala en Bosc, Cala en Bosc, tel: 971 380 600. Close to the marina, this large hotel has a pool and a restaurant. €€€
La Quinta, Carrer des Port s/n, tel: 971 387 014. A new spa hotel in a colonial-style building, not far from the beaches of Son Xoriguer and Cala en Bosc. Large outdoor pool, heated indoor pool and Turkish bath; water massage treatments. €€€

Cala en Forcat

Almirante Farragut, Cala en Forcat, tel: 971 388 000. Good service and comfortable rooms, many with sea views, in a hotel that sits above the long bay. Evening entertainment. €€

Cala N'Porter

Aquarium, Passeig de la Platja, tel: 971 377 077, fax: 971 377 337. Large and rather featureless but right on the beach, whereas many of the hotels here involve a long trek up the hill. €€

Cala Santa Galdana

Audax, tel: 971 154 646, fax: 971 154 647. Large and modern, close to sea and pine woods. Gym, sauna. €€€
Cala Galdana, Passeig Marítim, tel: 971 154 500, fax: 971 154 526. Large, efficient but impersonal hotel. Also an apartment-bungalow complex. €€€
Sol Gavilanes, tel: 971 15 45 45, fax: 971 154 546. Enormous, high-rise hotel above the bay; comfortable, good service, great views. €€€

Ciutadella

Ciutadella, Carrer Sant Eloi 10, tel: 971 383 462. Simple hotel near the Plaça Alfons III; most rooms with bath/shower; a restaurant with good Menorcan cuisine. €

Esmeralda, Passeig Sant Nicolau 171, tel: 971 380 250, fax: 971 380 258. Sinuous lines and blue balconies, with views of the harbour entrance; there's a pool and a tennis court. Family-oriented and mostly, but not exclusively, booked by tour groups. €

Hespería Patricia, Passeig San Nicolau 90–92, tel: 971 385 511, fax: 971 481 120. Modern, well-appointed hotel in a quiet position overlooking the port a few minutes' from Plaça del Born. Small pool. Also caters to business travellers. €€–€€€

Hostal Madrid, Carrer Madrid 60, tel: 971 380 328; fax: 971 482 158. Restaurant, small pool and garden. Not far from the town centre. Basic and friendly.

Hotel Rural Sant Ignasi, Carretera Cala Morell, tel: 971 385 575, fax: 971 480 529. An elegant, 18th-century manor house just 4km (2 1/2 miles) north of town. Excellent restaurant, and antique-furnished rooms. €€

Oasis, Carrer Sant Isidre 33, tel: 971 382 197. Close to the centre. Built around a courtyard, and has a bar and restaurant. Good value. €

Es Mercadal

Hostal Jeni, Mirador del Toro 81, tel: 971 375 059, fax: 971 375 124. This *hostal* offers simple but comfortable rooms in an ochre-coloured building near the town centre. There's a rooftop pool, and a good restaurant. €–€€

Es Migjorn Gran

S'Engolidor, Carrer Major 3, tel: 971 370 193. Stylish little establishment above a *barranc*, easy to miss because it's not signposted. Four simple guest rooms, antiques, quirky knick-knacks and excellent Menorcan cuisine. €–€€

Ferreries

Agroturismo Binisaid, Carretera Ferreries–Cala Santa Galdana Km 4.5, tel: 971 352 303. South of Ferreries and only 3km (2 miles) from the beach this attractive rural hotel has a small pool and just six double rooms. €

Son Triay Nou, Carretera Santa Galdana Km 3; tel: 971 155 078, fax: 971 360 446. Colonial style building, about 3km (2 miles) from Ferreries. A relaxing place to stay and a good starting point for walks in the nearby Barranc d'Algendar. Extensive grounds, pool and tennis court. Breakfast usually includes sausages and cheese made on the premises. €

Fornells

Hostal Fornells, Carrer Major 17, tel: 971 376 676; fax: 971 376 688. Attractive and friendly hotel which advertises itself as an 'eco resort'. Excellent breakfasts. Exercise and nutrition programmes can be arranged. Small pool and secluded terrace. €€

Hostal La Palma, Plaça S'Algaret 3, tel: 971 376 487, fax: 971 376 634. Right by the harbour, a friendly place with simply-furnished rooms, some overlooking the sea, others the little garden and pool. Busy local bar on ground floor. €

Hostal S'Algaret Plaça S'Algaret 7, tel: 971 376 552/971 376 666, fax: 971 376 499. Functional, plain and pleasant rooms, and a small pool. Harbour views from the first-floor restaurant's huge windows. €

Residencia Port Fornells, Ses Salines, tel: 971 376 373, fax: 971 376 634. Situated south of the town on the lagoon it is popular with sailors and windsurfers. €€

Maó and Es Castell

Almirante, Carretera Maó–Es Castell, tel: 971 362 700, fax: 971 362 704. Friendly, old-fashioned hotel in a Georgian mansion built for Nelson's right-hand man, Lord Collingwood. Ten antique-furnished bedrooms and a lounge in the main hotel; 30 other rooms built hacienda-style around a pleasant garden and pool. Half way between Maó and Es Castell. €

Barceló Hamilton, Passeig Santa Agueda 6, Es Castell; tel: 971 362 050. Refurbished in 1995, this modern hotel by the harbour has 166 rooms, most with sea views; there's also a pool. Largely but not exclusively booked by tour groups. €€

Capri, Carrer Sant Esteve 8, tel: 971 361 400. Modern, efficient and comfortable if somewhat lacking in character. Close to Plaça de s'Esplanada, its pool has views over the city. €€

Miramar, Moll de Fonduco 44, tel: 971 362 900; fax: 971 351 240. West of the city, set into the cliffs, on the water's edge with large sun terrace. Good value if prices don't rise when the current renovation is completed. €

Port Mahon, Avinguda Fort de l'Eau 13, tel: 971 362 600, fax: 971 351 050. A long-established hotel, with comfortable rooms in a rusty-red colonial-style building. Excellent service. Pool and attractive gardens. At the upper end of this price range. €€€

Posada Orsi, Carrer Infanta 19, tel: 971 364 751, fax: 971 357 394. This small, efficient and central *hostal* is under new management, and has been redecorated with ethnic touches and a 'chill-out room'. Some rooms have own bathrooms, others are shared.

Punta Prima

Barcelo Pueblo Menorca, tel: 971 151 850. One of the largest hotels on Menorca, in one of the island's first holiday resorts. Geared towards mass tourism, it's inexpensive but often fully booked by tour operators in high season. Good for family holidays. €

Sant Lluís

Alcaufar Vell Agoturismo, Carretera Cala Alcaufar Km 7, tel: 971

151 874, fax: 971 151 797. A neo-classical baronial mansion in wooded countryside close to the coast and Maó. Family-run, it has a welcoming atmosphere. *Cuina menorquina* is served in the restaurant. €€

Biniarroca Hotel Rural, Carretera Sant Lluís–Es Castell, tel: 971 150 059, fax: 971 151 250. This 15th-century farmhouse has been lovingly converted into an elegant country hotel. Terrace bar, attractive pool, sun terraces, peaceful gardens and an award-winning restaurant. €€

Hostal Biniali, Carrer S'Uestra–Binibeca, tel: 971 151 724, fax: 971 150 352. Restored *finca* southwest of town; quiet, elegant, with pool, a large terrace and good restaurant. Book well in advance. €€€

Sant Tomàs

Santo Tomàs, Platja de Sant Tomàs, tel: 971 370 025, fax: 971 370 204. Modern hotel beside the beach, with a gym and watersports facilities. €€€

Son Bou

Son Valentín Menorca, Urbanización Torre Solí Nou, tel: 971 372 748. If you prefer to avoid Son Bou's high-rises, this pleasant 'aparthotel' set back from the sea and surrounded by pines is a good option. €€

Visitors with disabilities

Menorca is not perhaps the best place for people with reduced mobility, but things are gradually improving. An increasing number of hotels have wheelchair access and some user-friendly rooms. Naturally, these tend to be the large, modern establishments. For more information, consult the online magazine Disability View, Craven Publishing, 15–39 Durham Street, Kinning Park, Glasgow GW1 1BS, tel: 0141 419 0044, fax: 0141 419 0077, www.disabilityview.co.uk

INDEX